Dining In-Seattle

COOKBOOK

TITLES IN SERIES

Feasting in Atlanta
Dining In–Baltimore
Dining In–Boston
Dining In–Chicago, Vol. I
Dining In–Chicago, Vol. II
Dining In–Dallas
Dining In–Denver
Dining In–Hawaii
Dining In–Houston, Vol. I
Dining In–Houston, Vol. II
Dining In–Kansas City
Dining In–Los Angeles
Dining In–Milwaukee
Dining In–Minneapolis/St. Paul, Vol. I
Dining In–Minneapolis/St. Paul, Vol. II
Dining In–Monterey Peninsula
Feasting In New Orleans
Dining In–Philadelphia
Dining In–Phoenix
Dining In–Pittsburgh
Dining In–Portland
Dining In–St. Louis
Dining In–San Francisco
Dining In–Seattle, Vol. I
Dining In–Seattle, Vol. II
Dining In–Seattle, Vol. III
Dining In–Sun Valley
Dining In–Washington D.C.
Dining In–Toronto
Dining In-Vancouver B.C.

VOLUME III

Dining In-Seattle

COOKBOOK

A Collection of Gourmet Recipes for Complete Meals
from the Seattle Area's Finest Restaurants

GREGORAKIS
AND
LOTZKAR

Foreword by
LENNY WILKENS

Peanut Butter Publishing
Mercer Island, Washington

Cover photograph by Rusnak/Leonardo Photography
Cover design and illustrations by Neil Sweeney

ISBN 0-89716-112-2

CONTENTS

FOREWORD

Now that Seattle has emerged as a city with an international flavor, San Francisco is no longer the only city on the West Coast known for its innovative cosmopolitanism. Seattle's natural beauty is enhanced by its excellent cultural and entertainment opportunities, and not least by the variety and depth of its fine restaurants. When one travels as much as I do, one wants dining out to be a certainty rather than an experience. I can say without reservation that Seattle doesn't take a back seat to any city when it comes to excellent restaurants.

No matter what your taste is, Seattle can accommodate it. I have tasted Italian food from the East Coast to the West Coast and the next best thing to eating it in Italy is a night out at Il Bistro. For a more international cuisine, one might select the Adriatica, where the menu covers the eastern half of the Mediterranean. And when the French in me surfaces, there are many area restaurants to enjoy, including Les Copains. There I can get my favorite rack of lamb—no one can cook lamb the way the French do.

The restaurant industry continues to grow as the city of Seattle grows. Today's diner can find an explosion of new restaurants, as well as those with long-standing reputations. Downtown Seattle draws many people with its numerous events, and this brings out the selective diner. For years, one downtown favorite has been the Olympic Hotel. Now, as the Four Seasons Olympic, it offers elegant surroundings and international cuisine in its premier dining room, the Georgian.

Across Lake Washington, where I live, my two favorite places are Morgan's Lakeplace and the Cafe Juanita. But the suburbs are also coming alive with good restaurants; I can only touch the surface of what is available in the area. Both residents and visitors now find dining out in Seattle a "certainty" for sure.

And with *Dining In–Seattle, Volume III*, we can find dining in a certainty, too. Imagine—twenty-two of the country's best restaurant meals, without leaving home. What a city, and what food!

Lenny Wilkens

Lenny Wilkens

ADRIATICA
CUCINA MEDITERRANEA

Dinner for Four

Asparagus or Leeks in Prosciutto with Herb Mayonnaise

John's Mostaccioli

Greek Potatoes

Costarelle

Vegetables Provençal

Dates and Walnuts in Fillo

Wine:

With the Asparagus and Mostaccioli—Grgich Hill Fumé Blanc, 1980

With the Costarelle—Taurasi, 1973 or Beaujolais, Morgon, 1978

Connie and Jim Malevetsis & John Sarich, Owners

ADRIATICA

The Adriatica is addictive: once there, you never want to leave; once gone, you want to go back. Much of this has to do with the familial sense about the place—the genuinely warm greetings offered by owners Connie and Jim Malevetsis and John Sarich (when he finds time to ascend from the downstairs kitchen) and the intimate, home-like setting the three have created at the restaurant. All this in combination with superb, authentically prepared Mediterranean-style cuisine makes for one of the most successful and popular restaurants in Seattle.

Greek-born Jim and Yugoslav-American John had been friends for years before the Adriatica came into being. John and Jim's wife Connie, with inspirational input from Jim, would prepare memorable feasts in the Mediterranean style at home. Over the platters of delicately prepared, uniquely seasoned delights, they would bemoan the lack of such fare in the Seattle restaurant world of that time. If they thought about being the ones to bring these pleasures before the city's dining public, however, it was only as a far-off dream—all were engaged in other professions which seemed to preclude the opening of a restaurant.

In November of 1979, Connie called everyone's bluff. She had found the perfect location for their fantasy restaurant. The home of the old Chez Paul, a lovely house close to the downtown area, had been sitting empty for a year. John's work had taken him to San Francisco; he was telephoned immediately and had moved back to Seattle almost before the line was dead. Negotiations proceeded rapidly and possession of the building was taken that January. More remarkably, after barely a month of frenetic work by friends and family, the Adriatica opened in mid-February to the acclaim of Seattle diners.

The menu epitomizes the simple, straightforward concepts on which the restaurant is based. Two or three seafood dishes, a pork item, a chicken piccata, *raznijici*—Yugoslavian marinated, grilled lamb—and two filet mignons, one basted in herb butter and the other sautéed with a mushroom/Marsala sauce, comprise the entrées. The calamari fritti appetizer, served with Greek skorthallia sauce and oozing with garlic, is by now a Seattle legend. The number of hors d'oeuvres, salads, soups, and pastas are kept to a minimum, each one thereby receiving the ultimate in preparation and presentation. And at the end, one has the choice of three desserts: *zuccotto*, a light Italian sponge cake; dates and walnuts in fillo pastry; and seasonal fresh fruit with white cheese and homemade crème fraîche.

1107 Dexter North

ADRIATICA

ASPARAGUS OR LEEKS IN PROSCIUTTO

Leeks and asparagus are equally delicious in this simple salad, depending which is in season or most readily available. Experiment with other vegetables, too—little would be ill-suited to this straightforward presentation.

1 to 1½ pounds fresh asparagus
(depending on size)
¼ pound high-quality
prosciutto, thinly sliced

HERB MAYONNAISE
(see next page)
Lemon slices (optional)

1. Trim off the thicker outer skin of the asparagus. Cut the stalks into even lengths. Tie together with kitchen string or wrap a band of aluminum foil around the bundle. Set the bundle, trimmed ends down, in a deep pot containing 1 inch of boiling salted water, to insure that the delicate tips are only steamed—not immersed—in water. Steam in this manner only until the asparagus turns bright green and is still quite crunchy.
2. Remove from the water, untie, and plunge into cold water to stop the cooking process and seal in the color and flavor. Dry thoroughly on a clean towel or paper towels.
3. Count the prosciutto slices. If the number will not make four equal portions, set aside any extra slices for other use. Spread the prosciutto slices with some of the Herb Mayonnaise. Place an equal portion of asparagus on each slice and roll into a bundle.
4. Place the bundles, evenly divided, among four salad plates. Spoon a dollop of Herb Mayonnaise atop each bundle, passing the remaining mayonnaise at the table should guests desire more sauce. Garnish with lemon slices, if desired.

Note: If using leeks, select young, tender stalks and cut off the greens at the point where they begin to be tough. Bring 2 to 3 quarts water to a boil in a pot; just before adding the whole leeks, add 1 tablespoon baking soda to the water (to help retain the green and tenderize the leeks). Boil until tender. Remove from water, plunge into cold water to stop the cooking process, dry thoroughly, and cut into halves or quarters lengthwise, depending on how large the leeks are. Proceed as with the asparagus.

Black Forest ham may be used in place of the prosciutto.

HERB MAYONNAISE

2 cups Mayonnaise
   (see index)
2 tablespoons Dijon-style
   mustard
3 tablespoons lemon juice
2 tablespoons chopped
   parsley

1 tablespoon fresh basil
   or ½ teaspoon dried
2 tablespoons capers,
   drained
¼ teaspoon dry tarragon
1 teaspoon chopped garlic
1 teaspoon minced shallot

In a blender, food processor, or by hand with a whisk or wooden spoon, thoroughly blend all ingredients. Let sit several hours or overnight so that the flavors meld.

JOHN'S MOSTACCIOLI

2 tablespoons butter
3 tablespoons olive oil,
   plus more as needed
2 large yellow onions,
   coarsely chopped
1 large green bell pepper,
   coarsely chopped
1 large red bell pepper,
   coarsely chopped
1 pound mushrooms,
   wiped clean and
   coarsely chopped
6 to 8 large, firm, ripe tomatoes,
   peeled, seeded, and
   coarsely chopped
2 tablespoons chopped garlic
½ cup dry white wine
2 tablespoons tomato paste

¼ cup chopped fresh basil,
   or 1 tablespoon dried
¼ cup chopped parsley
1 tablespoon chopped fresh
   oregano, or 1 teaspoon
   dried
⅛ teaspoon ground allspice
½ to 1 teaspoon crushed red
   pepper (optional)
2 pinches sugar
   Salt and pepper to taste
1 to 1½ cups Chicken Stock
   (as needed—see index)
1 pound mostaccioli pasta
1 pound fresh, creamy
   ricotta cheese
½ pound mozzarella, grated
   Chopped parsley

1. Place a skillet over high heat; add the butter and oil and as soon as the butter melts add the onions, peppers, and mushrooms. Cook, stirring constantly, until the vegetables are limp but not brown.
2. Add the tomatoes and garlic, then the wine. Stir thoroughly to blend ingredients. Add the tomato paste, herbs, sugar, and salt and pepper to taste. Stir again. Reduce heat to moderately low and simmer, covered, for about 5 minutes. If the mixture seems too dry, add a bit of the chicken stock—just enough to moisten; do not turn the mixture into soup. Taste again and correct seasoning, if desired. Set aside.
3. Preheat oven to 350°.
4. In a minimum of 6 quarts of water, cook the mostaccioli according to the package directions. Cook only until the pasta is al dente; there should be a touch of chewiness still remaining. (It will be cooked further in the oven.) Drain and rinse quickly under cold water to stop the cooking process. Toss vigorously in a colander to rid the pasta of most of the water.
5. Thoroughly combine the mostaccioli with the tomato mixture. Taste again and correct seasoning, if necessary.
6. Place the mixture in a buttered or oiled au gratin dish or appropriately sized ovenproof baking dish attractive enough to place on the table. Dot the top of the mixture with the ricotta. Sprinkle evenly with the grated mozzarella. Cover with aluminum foil and bake in preheated oven for 20 to 25 minutes, or until well heated and bubbly. Remove the foil for the last 5 minutes of baking to allow the cheese topping to harden slightly.
7. Let cool 10 to 15 minutes before serving. Sprinkle with chopped parsley.

This delicious pasta can be served as a meatless entrée for lunch or dinner or utilized as a side dish to accompany meat or poultry.

GREEK POTATOES

6 to 8 medium-size russet
    potatoes, scrubbed
    and dried
  ½ cup olive oil
    Peanut oil for deep-frying
    Salt

White pepper
Greek oregano
¼ cup freshly minced parsley,
    plus more to taste
Lemon slices (optional)

1. Cube the unpeeled potatoes into ½-inch pieces and soak in ice water for 30 minutes to rid the potatoes of excess starch. Drain the potatoes and dry well on clean tea towels or paper towels.

2. In a large skillet over moderately high heat, place the olive oil and let it get very hot. Add the potatoes and toss constantly with a metal spatula until the potatoes are just beginning to turn golden brown. At this point, remove them from the pan and lay them in one layer on a cookie sheet.

3. About 30 minutes before serving, place the potatoes on the cookie sheet in a slow 250° oven, just to keep warm (or to rewarm).

4. Just before serving, heat the peanut oil to 400°. Deep-fry the potatoes for approximately 30 seconds—just enough to give them a golden crust. Drain and place in a heated serving bowl or on a platter.

5. Sprinkle to taste with salt, white pepper, and Greek oregano. Add ¼ cup chopped parsley and toss thoroughly. Serve, garnished with more chopped parsley and lemon slices if desired.

We have experimented with many methods of preparing Greek fries. This three-part procedure is the one that accomplishes the precise result for which we were looking: a golden, crisp potato piece, succulent inside, almost appearing to have been baked in the oven.

COSTARELLE
Marinated, Grilled Pork T-Bone

2 tablespoons finely chopped garlic	Salt
¾ cup olive oil	Freshly ground black pepper
½ cup lemon juice	4 (1½"-thick) pork
½ cup dry white wine (preferably vermouth)	T-bone steaks
1 teaspoon thyme	Parsley sprigs
	Lemon wedges

1. Place the garlic, oil, lemon juice, wine, thyme, salt, and pepper in a bowl and whisk until the mixture congeals and thickens. Pour the mixture into a glass dish large enough to hold the steaks in one layer.
2. Place the steaks in the marinade, turning several times to thoroughly coat both sides. Let the steaks marinate for 3 to 4 hours at room temperature, turning at half-hour intervals.
3. Broil or, preferably, grill the steaks over hot, white coals for 20 minutes, turning every 5 minutes to produce a criss-cross pattern on both sides. The meat should be cooked a light grey, with a slight pinkness next to the bone.
4. Place on a large, heated serving platter or on individual heated plates. Garnish with parsley sprigs and lemon wedges.

If the steaks are overcooked, they will be dry and tough.

We purchase our pork T-bones at Don and Joe's Meats in Seattle's Pike Place Market, where you may ask for them cut "à la Adriatica." Elsewhere, simply request the pork steak cut with the loin and tenderloin left attached to the T-bone.

VEGETABLES PROVENÇAL

6 to 8 (6"-long) firm zucchini,
  scrubbed and dried
⅓ cup olive oil
1 cup coarsely chopped
  onion
2 tablespoons finely chopped
  garlic
2 cups peeled, seeded,
  and chopped tomatoes

⅓ cup dry white wine
¼ cup chopped fresh basil,
  or 2 teaspoons dried
¼ cup chopped fresh
  parsley
Salt
Freshly ground black
  pepper

1. Julienne the zucchini into 2-inch by ¼-inch strips. Heat the olive oil in a skillet over high heat. Add the zucchini strips and toss them constantly to insure even cooking. When the strips begin to get tender (3 to 4 minutes), add the onion, tomato, and garlic, continuing to stir until the onion is wilted and the tomato begins to break down.
2. Add the white wine. Stir and then add the basil, parsley, and salt and pepper to taste. Stir well and let the liquid begin to evaporate.
3. Reduce heat to low, cover the skillet, and let the mixture simmer for about 3 minutes. Taste again; correct seasoning if necessary. Place on a heated serving platter or in a heated bowl and serve.

This method of vegetable preparation is equally adaptable to green beans, broccoli, cauliflower, and small yellow summer squash. For texture and color variety, mix various vegetables.

DATES AND WALNUTS IN FILLO

2 cups shelled walnuts
6 cups pitted dates
½ cup good cognac
5 leaves fillo dough, at room
    temperature

½ pound butter, melted
Lightly sweetened whipped
    cream

1. Process the walnuts and dates in a food processor fitted with a steel blade. When the mixture begins to stick, add the cognac. When the mixture is of a gooey, rather muddy consistency, stop mixing.
2. Refrigerate the mixture for a minimum of 1 hour or as much as 2 or 3 days, or until thoroughly chilled.
3. When chilled, remove from the refrigerator and, with your hands, roll the date/walnut mixture into long cigars no more than ½ inch in diameter. Cut the cigars into lengths as long as your index finger.
4. Carefully remove the fillo from the plastic bag and lay the pile out flat. Layer 5 sheets of fillo, one on top of the other, buttering well between each layer. Butter the top layer. Cut the sheets lengthwise in half and then twice across the width of the fillo, producing six even squares.
5. Lay 1 date/walnut cigar across the square at the end closest to you. Fold the sides over and roll up the date/walnut cigar in the fillo, producing another cigar-shaped roll. Butter the ends of the fillo and press lightly so that the ends stay closed. Repeat for the remaining squares.
6. Place 1 inch apart on a cookie sheet covered with waxed paper. Refrigerate for at least 1 hour (or for up to a week, covered with plastic wrap). The rolls may also be frozen at this point (in which case they can be put directly into the oven when you wish to cook them— although they may require a bit more cooking time).
7. When ready to bake, place in a preheated 500° oven and bake for 5 to 8 minutes, or until the top is nicely browned and the cigars are puffed. Top with whipped cream and serve while warm.

These are also good at room temperature and can make a delicious picnic dessert.

Annie et Robert

Dinner for Four

Magura Sashimi

Japanese Vegetable Salad

Feuilleté St. Jacques aux Truffes et au Vin de Prune

Pink Bananas au Gratin

Beverages:

With the Sashimi—dry saké or Japanese beer

With the Salad—Riesling, Johannisberg Klaus, Rhemigan, 1979

With the Scallops—Chablis Premier Cru, Bichot, 1978
or
Chateau St. Jean Chardonnay, Robert Young Vineyard, 1979

With the Bananas—Schramsberg Blanc de Blancs
or
Louis Roederer N.V. Brut

Annie Agostini, Owner

Didier Quincampoix & Masa M. Akimoto, Chefs

ANNIE ET ROBERT

At Annie et Robert, mirrored columns accented with brass ribbons, grey-brown walls, red brick floors, white table linen, Oriental screens, and potted plants provide a setting to complement the cuisine: crisp, sleek, and stunning. When the restaurant opened in June, 1981, many eyebrows were raised at the notion of combining Japanese and French nouvelle cuisines under one roof. It is not such an unlikely idea, however. Many classic French chefs have made treks to Japan over the years to study and observe culinary techniques, and likewise have Japanese chefs often served apprenticeships in France. For at heart the two cuisines embody almost identical sets of values: quintessentially fresh ingredients cooked with uncompromising perfectionism and presented in elegant, artistic simplicity.

Annie Agostini (who is also proprietor of Crêpe de Paris) however, has a further goal: to create, through the genius and magic of French and Japanese masters working together in her kitchen, a new cuisine that combines the best of both worlds' ingredients, techniques, and presentation. Although Annie feels that the goal is still evolving, wonders have already been accomplished. The "French" side of the East/West menu reveals an apparent Oriental influence, from sole laced with plum wine and salmon-roe sauce to crêpes filled with scallops and shiitake mushrooms in sesame sauce.

The menu changes daily. The raw materials in use are consistent, but the manner in which they are prepared and presented is in a constant creative flux. Chefs Akimoto and Quincampoix work side by side to develop the progression of cross-cultural inspiration. An appreciable effort has been made to connect with the best food producers and vendors; because part of the restaurant houses a classic sushi bar, particular attention is given to the selection of all seafood.

117 Pine

ANNIE ET ROBERT

MAGURA SASHIMI

¼ to ½ pound fresh Hawaiian
        tuna
¼ ounce wasabi
½ cup pickled ginger

1 daikon radish
½ cup soy sauce

1. Slice the tuna approximately ¼ inch thick to produce six slices per person. Arrange artistically on a simple, plain dish.
2. Form the wasabi into the shape of a leaf and place it next to the tuna on the plate.
3. Arrange a little pile of ginger on one corner of the plate.
4. Finely julienne the daikon radish and arrange it on the opposite side of the ginger.
5. Divide the soy sauce between four small bowls. To serve, place the tuna plate in the center of the table, with the bowls of soy sauce at each setting. Guests then place a bit of the wasabi into the soy and dip the tuna into the mixture. The daikon is used as a pleasant accompaniment to the tuna and the ginger is used to cleanse the palate between bites.

The quality and freshness of the tuna is imperative for this dish. If you do not have an on-going relationship with a reputable fishmonger, seek out the advice of an expert who does.

Wasabi is a hot horseradish preparation which may be purchased at Oriental markets.

ANNIE ET ROBERT

JAPANESE VEGETABLE SALAD

1 daikon radish, washed
   and scrubbed
1 stalk celery
2 green onions
2 small red onions
4 carrots, peeled

¼ cup sesame seeds
1 lotus root
2 tablespoons saké
¼ cup soy sauce
½ cup rice vinegar
¾ teaspoon wasabi

1. Julienne the daikon, celery, green onions, red onions, and carrots. Arrange the vegetables on four round plates in a circular pattern, with the julienned strips pointing toward the center.
2. Place the sesame seeds in the center of each salad.
3. Slice the lotus root thinly and garnish each serving with one slice.
4. Combine the saké, soy sauce, rice vinegar, and wasabi. Mix well. Pass the dressing in a separate sauceboat or small pitcher or provide a small portion of it to each guest in an individual serving container.

FEUILLETÉ ST. JACQUES AU TRUFFES ET AU VIN DE PRUNE
Scallops in Pastry with Truffles and Plum Wine

6 ounces puff pastry dough
1 egg yolk, beaten
24 fresh scallops
1 cup flour
7 tablespoons butter
3 ounces truffles, julienned
1 tablespoon truffle juice
7 ounces fresh cream

⅔ cup Japanese plum wine
Salt
Freshly ground white
   pepper to taste
1 daikon radish, julienned
½ pound snow peas
Watercress

1. Preheat oven to 375°.
2. Roll out the puff pastry dough into a square, ⅛-inch thick. Cut the large square into 4 equal smaller squares.
3. Place the four squares on a flat baking pan and brush with the beaten egg yolk. Bake in preheated oven for 20 minutes. Remove from the oven and cut the squares through the middle horizontally. Reserve the pastries on the pan; keep warm by the oven.

4. While the pastries are baking, dredge the scallops in the flour. Heat 4 tablespoons butter in a skillet over moderately high heat. Add the scallops and sauté for 2 minutes at the most (even less for very small scallops). Place the skillet off the heat but close to the oven to keep warm.

5. In a separate skillet or enameled saucepan, melt 1 tablespoon butter. Add the truffles and truffle juice and cook over medium heat to reduce the liquid by half. Add the cream and plum wine and reduce again by half. Add salt and pepper to taste.

6. Place the scallops in the sauce and heat on low for just 1 minute, so as not to overcook.

7. Melt the remaining 2 tablespoons butter in a separate pan over high heat. Add the daikon and snow peas and sauté briefly.

8. Divide the scallop mixture evenly onto the bottom half of each of the four cut puff-pastry squares. Place the top halves back on. Serve on heated plates with a small bouquet of watercress and the daikon/pea mixture.

PINK BANANAS AU GRATIN

1 tablespoon butter	4 pink bananas, cut in
3 tablespoons powdered	half lengthwise
sugar	1 ounce Japanese vodka
¼ cup apricot jam	8 leaves fresh mint

1. Preheat oven to 350°.

2. Melt the butter with the sugar in a saucepan or skillet. Cook over moderate heat until the mixture turns a light caramel color. At this point, stir in the apricot jam until it is melted and well combined.

3. Add the split bananas. Cook 2 minutes over low heat, turning often in the syrupy mixture.

4. Add the vodka, gently heat, and ignite with a match. When the flames subside, put the bananas in ramekin dishes. Pour sauce evenly over each portion and place a mint leaf on each serving.

5. Bake in preheated oven for 2 minutes only. Serve hot.

Pink bananas are available at specialty stores.

Avenue 52
٥٢ أفنيو

Dinner for Four

Baba Ghanouj

Upside-Down Chicken

Mediterranean Salad

Cantaloupe-Chocolate Ice Cream Parfaits

Arabian Coffee

Wine:

Pinot Grìgio, J. Brigl,
or
Mâcon-Lugny Chardonnay,
or
Simi Chardonnay

Saleh Joudeh, Owner & Chef

The uncommon blend of classical Middle Eastern and Italian cuisines often surprises first-time diners at the Avenue 52, but interest replaces surprise when they discover how the restaurant evolved. Formerly the historic Hasty Tasty of upper University Avenue, the Avenue 52 opened May 11, 1979 to serve hamburgers which owner and chef Saleh Joudeh had made legendary during his stint at the Greenlake Bowl Cafe. Popularity of the hamburgers ensured the success of the new restaurant. Soon after its opening, however, patrons discovered that Saleh could prepare delightful dishes familiar to him from his childhood in Damascus and his many years spent in Perugia, Italy. As his Mediterranean fare garnered kudos from Seattle diners, the hamburgers gradually disappeared from the menu, and the restaurant's atmosphere changed. Today, the Avenue 52 with its candles and white linen is an intimate, romantic spot where emphasis is on authentic meals prepared from first-rate, fresh ingredients.

Much attention is given to subtle seasoning and true representation of foods from both Italy and the Middle East. The pasta is made fresh daily and is served only with light sauces cooked to each guest's satisfaction. The hummos and baba ghanouj, favored Middle Eastern appetizers, are made in the traditional, time-consuming manner. Before being peeled, for instance, the eggplants in the baba ghanouj are hand-broiled one by one over a gas flame. Kebabs are always fork-tender, because the Washington-grown lamb is cut on the premises. And the beef tenderloin, the best available, is sliced for each order to maintain the utmost freshness and flavor. In fact, one of the primary reasons for keeping the menu small but well rounded is to offer the guest consistently delectable dishes prepared to perfection from the choicest of ingredients.

The knowledge and sensitivity of the staff exemplifies Saleh's policy of attention given to every detail that makes dining at Avenue 52 memorable. The staff pointedly recall names, faces, and candid comments which are always encouraged.

5247 University Way NE

BABA GHANOUJ

2 medium-size eggplant
6 cloves garlic
  Juice of 3 to 4 lemons
    (approximately ¾ cup)
2 teaspoons salt

1 cup tahini (sesame butter)
2 to 3 tablespoons olive oil
  Chopped parsley
  Pita bread

1. Make two deep slits in each eggplant to facilitate venting when cooking. Insert a long fork or skewer into the end of each and cook over an open gas flame or hot charcoals, turning occasionally, until all surfaces are very black and charred.

2. Cool the eggplant under cold running water, then carefully peel away the blackened skin and discard. With a sharp French knife, finely chop the pulp to the consistency of purée. Transfer this to a large bowl.

3. Mash the garlic with the side of a knife until puréed and add to the eggplant. Add the lemon juice, salt, and sesame butter. Beat vigorously with a wire whisk until well blended. A touch of water may be needed to facilitate the blending. Taste to adjust seasonings.

4. To serve, spread the Baba Ghanouj onto a large platter to about ½-inch thickness, making a slight circular depression in the center. Pour 2 to 3 tablespoons olive oil into the depression and garnish with chopped parsley. Serve with warm pita bread to dip into the mixture.

Note: The eggplant can be charred under the broiler of an oven if gas flames or charcoal are not available. The Baba Ghanouj, however, will not have quite the classical smoky flavor if done this way.

UPSIDE-DOWN CHICKEN

1 *chicken*	1 *tablespoon salt*
1 *medium head cauliflower*	5 *tablespoons butter*
1½ *cups vegetable oil*	¼ *teaspoon cumin*
2 *cups long-grain white*	6 to 8 *cloves garlic*
rice	⅓ *cup pine nuts*
¼ *teaspoon allspice*	*YOGURT SAUCE*

1. Boil the whole chicken in water to cover until the chicken is nearly done, about 1 hour. The juices should run pink when the thigh is pricked with a fork. Remove the chicken and cool; strain the broth and reserve. Remove the meat from the bones.

2. Cut the cauliflower into small florets. In a heavy skillet, heat the vegetable oil until hot but not smoking. Fry the cauliflower until golden. Drain on paper towels.

3. Soak the rice in cold water to cover for 15 minutes. Drain.

4. Combine 2 cups reserved chicken broth with the allspice and 2 teaspoons salt and bring to a boil.

5. In a 4-quart dutch oven with straight sides and handles lower than the rim, melt 2 tablespoons butter over moderately high heat. Arrange the chicken meat on the bottom of the pan, then layer with the cauliflower and sprinkle with the cumin and the remaining 1 teaspoon salt. Scatter the whole garlic cloves over. Cover with the uncooked rice and pour the boiling stock over all.

6. Bring to a boil and reduce heat to low. Cover and continue cooking until the rice is tender and the liquid has been absorbed, about 20 minutes. Remove from heat.

7. In a small saucepan, melt 3 tablespoons butter over moderate heat and, stirring constantly, brown the pine nuts.

8. Place a heated, round platter securely over the top of the dutch oven and, using both hands, carefully flip the pan upside down onto the plate. Gently tap the bottom and slowly remove the pan to retain the circular shape. Pour the browned butter and pine nuts around the top. Serve with Yogurt Sauce and/or Mediterranean Salad.

This mélange is an original recipe and is one of my most popular dishes. It is relatively simple to make at home and provides an unusual, enjoyable treat for guests.

YOGURT SAUCE

2 cloves garlic
1 pound plain yogurt
1 large cucumber,
   peeled and diced

2 teaspoons dried Middle-
   Eastern mint, or
8 leaves fresh mint,
   chopped

Mash the garlic to a purée with the side of a knife. Place all ingredients in a bowl and mix thoroughly.

The flavor of this sauce will be best if made a day ahead, or at least several hours before eating. It is served here as a condiment with the Upside-Down Chicken, but it is also delicious with fried or poached fish—particularly salmon.

MEDITERRANEAN SALAD

4 ripe, firm tomatoes
2 green onions
2 radishes (red or white)
1 head romaine lettuce,
   washed and thoroughly
   dried, tough outer
   leaves discarded
1 medium-size cucumber,
   peeled
½ cup chopped fresh parsley

½ teaspoon dried Middle-
   Eastern mint, or 5 to 6
   fresh mint leaves,
   finely chopped
Salt
Pepper
¼ cup olive oil
¼ cup freshly squeezed
   lemon juice

1. Cut the tomatoes, green onions, radishes, lettuce, and cucumber into small pieces (approximately ½-inch cubes or pieces). Place in a large salad bowl. Add the parsley and mint.
2. Add the salt, pepper, olive oil, and lemon juice. Mix well and taste for seasoning. Add more salt, lemon, or mint if desired.

CANTALOUPE-CHOCOLATE ICE CREAM PARFAITS

1 ripe cantaloupe

1 quart chocolate ice cream

With a melon baller, remove the pulp from the cantaloupe. In chilled parfait or large wine glasses, alternately layer the balls of melon with balls of ice cream. Serve immediately with Arabian Coffee.

ARABIAN COFFEE

4   teaspoons white sugar
8   teaspoons Arabian coffee

¼   teaspoon ground
     cardamom

1. Place 4 demitasse cups of water and the sugar in a small saucepan or Middle-Eastern handled coffee maker. Bring to a boil.
2. Take the water/sugar mixture off the heat and add the coffee and cardamom.
3. Return to heat. Let the mixture come to a boil three times, each time pulling it off the heat to subside just as it begins to boil.
4. Pour into demitasse cups and serve.

If Arabian coffee is not available, another dark-roast coffee ground very, very fine will suffice—but it should be a finer grind than espresso.

il Bistro

Dinner for Four

Prawns Aglio
or
Il Bistro Mussel Sauté

Linguini Sardegna

Braciole

Lemon Sorbet

Beverages:

With the Prawns or Mussels and Linguini—Montagny

With the Braciole—Barolo, Cavalotto, 1971

With or after the Sorbet—Cognac, Ragnaud Estate-bottled

Peter Lamb & Frank Daquila, Owners

Frank Daquila, Head Chef

David Dorn, Executive Chef

IL BISTRO

O ne walks into Il Bistro off Post Alley and senses the charm of entering a cafe from a street in a European city. Inside, vestiges of the Old World beckon enticingly: a rich mahogany bar, stained wood floors, creamy off-white stucco, gentle arches and curves, exposed brick, colorful kilims, and a stunning center wine table. The mood is sustained as diners are left alone to linger over food, wine and conversation, yet not feel neglected. Peter Lamb, who with Frank Daquila founded Il Bistro, insists on the expert service that heightens this intimacy: "People are coming to dine leisurely in an unpretentious but real setting—not to see the waiters."

When Peter and Frank first joined forces in 1975, their restaurant was located on the ground floor of the Harbor Heights building, now the site of Market Place North. The kitchen was makeshift, the decor less than stunning, and the menu limited. Even so, the simple, impeccably prepared food and terrific wines-by-the-glass became the talk of the town. Since its move to Pike Street in 1977, the bistro has continued to grow in the limelight of Seattle's best dining spots.

From the onset, Frank wanted the food at Il Bistro to embody the best of the lighter, more delicate Northern Italian cuisine with overtones of the zing typical of his native Abruzzi, and generally accomplished by the precise use of hot red pepper. Thus, red sauces and marinades have just the right touch of piquancy without detracting from the natural foods they accent.

Executive chef David Dorn, who has worked closely with Frank, shares the owner's vision of the food's ethnic style, its presentation, and the careful selection of quality ingredients. Guests are introduced to appetizers such as succulent seafood antipasto, creamy pasta, superbly sautéed prawns, or an elegant platter of prosciutto and melon. Entrées include a spicy cioppino, veal Marsala and Parmigiana (the scallopini are cut from the choicest rib eye), a tenderloin medallion sauté, and at least two pasta/seafood mélanges that melt in the mouth. Vegetables are not overlooked. Simple accomaniments, perfectly cooked, provide pleasing contrasts in color, flavor, and texture.

93-A Pike Street

PRAWNS AGLIO
Prawns Sautéed in Olive Oil and Garlic

1 *pound shrimp*	*Juice of 1 lemon*
¼ *cup olive oil*	¼ *cup dry white vermouth*
3 *large cloves garlic,*	*(approximately)*
finely minced	1 *tablespoon butter*
½ *teaspoon oregano*	*Parsley sprigs*
Salt and pepper to taste	*Lemon wedges*

1. Devein the shrimp with the shells on by running the blade of a small, sharp scissor down the back of the shrimp through the shell and pulling the vein out. Rinse and dry well with paper towels.
2. Heat the olive oil over high heat in a sauté pan large enough to comfortably hold all the shrimp without crowding. When the oil is hot, add the garlic and quickly stir about in the oil, taking care not to burn.
3. Immediately add the shrimp. Stir constantly. Add the oregano, a generous pinch of salt, and a generous amount of freshly ground pepper. Be sure that the garlic does not burn. As the shrimp turn pink (2 to 3 minutes), add the lemon juice. Stir thoroughly.
4. Cook only until the shrimp are pink and resilient to the touch, no more than 3 to 4 minutes. If overcooked, shrimp are tough. Place on a heated platter or individual heated serving dishes.
5. Quickly pour the vermouth into the pan, still over high heat. Let reduce by half. Add a dash of butter and a sprinkling of black pepper. Taste for seasoning and pour evenly over the shrimp. Garnish with fresh parsley and lemon wedges.

Provide your guests with large bibs and/or wet towels, for the quality of this dish is impaired if the shrimp are cooked without their shells.

Use either large (16 to 20-count per pound) or medium (25 to 32-count) shrimp. Since virtually all shrimp available in our markets have been frozen, be sure to purchase those that have been thawed only on the day you buy them, for if they have been in the case longer than that, noticeable textural and flavor damage occurs.

IL BISTRO MUSSEL SAUTÉ

1 bunch fresh basil	3 to 4 pounds fresh Atlantic
¼ cup olive oil	mussels, de-bearded
8 to 10 cloves garlic,	and scrubbed
finely minced	½ cup red wine vinegar
1 teaspoon dry oregano	Freshly ground pepper
1 pound ripe Roma or	and salt to taste
other fresh tomatoes,	Freshly minced parsley
peeled, seeded, and diced	French bread

1. Wash the basil. Remove the stems. Dry the leaves with paper towels and mince.
2. Heat the oil in a large sauté pan over moderately high heat. Add the garlic, oregano and basil. Stir briskly. Just as the garlic begins to turn golden brown, add the tomatoes.
3. Cook the tomatoes, stirring constantly, for 1 minute. Add the mussels. Stir the mussels several times, turning them in the tomato mixture until they begin to open. Add the vinegar.
4. Place a lid on the pan and cook the mussels until they have completely opened. As soon as they have opened, cook 1 to 2 minutes and then remove with a slotted spoon to a heated platter. Discard any that do not open. Cover loosely with foil.
5. Reduce the liquid in the pan over high heat for 3 to 4 minutes, or until reduced by half. Add salt and pepper to taste.
6. Pour the liquid over the mussels, sprinkle with the minced parsley, and serve with crusty French bread.

Because of the vinegar, this dish is as good at room temperature as it is warm.

LINGUINI SARDEGNA

1 pint heavy cream
½ cup half and half
1 cup FRESH TOMATO SAUCE (see next page)
1 pound Dungeness crabmeat
1 cup freshly grated Pecorino Romano cheese

1 pound egg or spinach linguini
¼ pound freshly grated Parmesan cheese (preferably Parmigiano-Reggiano)
Freshly minced parsley

1. Place the heavy cream and half and half in an enameled pan and, stirring constantly over moderately high heat, reduce the mixture until it reaches the consistency of lightly whipped cream—slightly thick and frothy.
2. Add the Fresh Tomato Sauce to the reduced cream mixture and reduce again by half over slightly lower heat.
3. Add the fresh crabmeat. When it is heated through, add the Pecorino Romano and stir until the cheese is melted.
4. Cook the linguini in 6 to 7 quarts of boiling, salted water until resistant to the bite, not mushy. Fresh linguini will only take approximately 1 minute to cook; dried, no more than 5 minutes.
5. Drain the pasta quickly and immediately place in a heated bowl. Toss the tomato/crab mixture into the pasta with swift moves of special pasta forks or other large forks and add the Parmesan while tossing.
6. Serve immediately on heated plates or in heated bowls. Sprinkle with minced parsley.

Note: The only trick to making successful pasta dishes is to be organized, because once the pasta hits the water, the dish is near completion. Before making a quick pasta sauce, be sure to turn the pasta water on high, as it will take 10 to 15 minutes for it to boil. Have your tossing and serving bowls or plates heated, as pasta cools quickly enough as it is. As importantly, get your guests organized and ready to eat before adding the pasta to the water.

With succulent Dungeness crab available in this area, Linguini Sardegna takes on a special essence. Other types of crab could be used. The combination of fresh cream, reduced to a velvety consistency, and tasty homemade tomato sauce contributes to the rich yet clean flavor of this dish.

IL BISTRO

FRESH TOMATO SAUCE

5 pounds fresh ripe pear
  tomatoes
1 bunch fresh basil, leaves
  removed from stems,
  rinsed, dried with paper
  towels and finely minced
2 tablespoons olive oil

1 small onion, finely
  chopped
8 to 10 cloves garlic, finely
  minced
½ cup dry white wine
  Salt and freshly ground
  pepper to taste

1. Cut the stem tips from the tomatoes. Place in a large pan with water to cover. Cover and bring to a boil over high heat. Cook until the skins crack, about 4 to 5 minutes.
2. Drain in a colander. Rinse with cold water, then squeeze the pulp out of the skins and into a bowl. Crush by hand and set aside.
3. Pluck the basil leaves from the stems and rinse. Dry with paper towels. Mince finely.
4. Heat a heavy-bottomed saucepan over high heat. Add the oil and allow to heat. Add the onion, garlic, and basil and sauté for 3 to 4 minutes.
5. Add the wine and cook 1 to 2 minutes. Add the crushed tomatoes and salt and pepper to taste. Continue cooking over moderately high heat for 10 to 15 minutes.

This sauce should have a fresh, clean taste, sufficiently salted, but not heavily spiced. Use the extra sauce in other Italian or fresh vegetable dishes immediately or freeze in small containers and use as needed.

BRACIOLE
Stuffed Beef Roll

1 *(2 to 2½-pound) round*
  steak, butterflied
Grated rind of 1 lemon
Salt and pepper
2½ *teaspoons oregano*
¼ *pound prosciutto,*
  thinly sliced
2 *cups bread crumbs*
¼ *pound Parmigiano-*
  Reggiano cheese, grated
½ *cup chopped parsley*

½ *teaspoon rosemary*
½ *cup flour*
¼ *cup olive oil*
4 *cloves garlic, finely*
  chopped
1 *small onion, diced*
½ *cup dry red wine*
2 *cups chopped, canned*
  pear tomatoes
  with their juice

1. Open the butterflied steak and, with waxed paper covering it, pound evenly with a meat mallet until approximately ¼ inch thick. Rub the lemon rind, salt, pepper, and 1½ teaspoons oregano into the meat.
2. Lay the prosciutto slices evenly on the steak. Sprinkle the bread crumbs, grated Parmesan, and parsley evenly over the prosciutto slices.
3. Roll the braciole tightly, taking care while rolling to tuck in both ends so as to hold in the filling while cooking. Tie the roll with strings at 1½ to 2-inch intervals.
4. Rub the rosemary between your palms to break it up. Season the flour with the rosemary, remaining oregano, and salt and pepper. Rub this mixture onto the surface of the beef roll.
5. In a pan large enough to hold the roll, heat the olive oil over moderately high heat. Add the beef roll, turning to brown the entire surface.
6. Add the garlic and onion and cook until the garlic begins to turn golden brown. Add the wine and cook for 1 minute.
7. Add the tomatoes with their juice and salt and pepper to taste. Cover the pan and simmer over low heat for 1 to 1½ hours, or until very tender when pierced with a fork. If liquid appears to be diminishing during the cooking, splash a bit more wine into the pan.

(continued next page)

8. Remove from the pan and place on a heated platter. Remove the strings, cut into ½-inch thick slices, pour the tomato mixture over the slices, and serve.

Note: If serving cold, place the braciole on a platter, pour the sauce over it, cover tightly with plastic wrap or foil, and refrigerate. Before serving, bring to room temperature, remove the strings, and cut into slices as mentioned above. The slices can be served on a bed of lettuce, accompanied by freshly baked bread.

This scrumptious roll is equally good hot or cold.

LEMON SORBET

1½ cups fresh lemon juice	1 tablespoon grated
3 cups SIMPLE SYRUP	lemon zest

Combine the ingredients and freeze in an ice-cream maker. Alternatively, place in a bowl set within a larger bowl holding ice cubes and salted water. Beat the mixture with a portable mixer or wire whisk for several minutes until it begins to be thoroughly chilled. Cover and place in the freezer until frozen, stirring occasionally.

IL BISTRO

SIMPLE SYRUP

2 *cups sugar*   4 *cups water*

Place the sugar and water in a stainless steel or enameled saucepan and boil for 5 minutes. Strain through a sieve lined with a damp cloth. Cool.

CAFE JUANITA

Dinner for Four

Insalata di Frutti di Mare

Spaghettini with Smoked Salmon

Pan-Braised Sea Bass

Mixed Fresh Vegetables with Parmesan Cheese

Cafe Juanita Green Salad with Herbed Vinaigrette

Spuma di Cioccolata

Beverages:

*As an apéritif or with the Insalata or Spaghettini—
Italian Spumanti Cartizze or Pro Secco*

With the Insalata and Spaghettini—Orvieto Classico, Decugano dei Barbi

With the Sea Bass—Pinot Grìgio, J. Brigl

With the Cioccolata—Vin Santo

Peter Dow, Proprietor

David Hepburn, Chef

CAFE JUANITA

Peter Dow, proprietor of the Cafe Juanita and long-standing restaurateur in the Seattle area, wants people to have fun when they come to his dining establishment. Considering his own experiences in Italy, in combination with his already existing personal philosophy about eating, Peter encourages "life and fun at the Italian table—eating a meal is more than just dining; it is an event where people converse, laugh, and relax." This attitude is combined with the absolute commitment to quality and simplicity: simplicity in the decor, in the service, and in the food. The current site, an old house that Peter describes before remodeling as "early ugly Bellevue," is warm and comforting in its clean, crisp presentation.

The Cafe Juanita had humble beginnings in 1978 in a small and "very funky" location that now houses the Juanita Bay Racketball Club. The original cafe, serving only breakfast and lunch, was in essence just an extension of Peter's famous Gordo's hamburger stand, which he owned at that time. In 1979, Peter began researching and experimenting with Northern Italian food. Soon scrambled eggs at breakfast were replaced with fresh pasta and pollo ai pistacci for dinner. Lasagne followed, and then a fresh fish daily special. Then came an enthusiastic review in the *Argus* and, by the autumn of 1979, Peter Dow had an earthy but tremendously successful little Italian restaurant. With a seating capacity of twenty-eight, he worked up until two days before the building was razed in June 1981.

Soon after, Peter traveled to Italy to observe cooking and eating styles. When he returned and shortly opened the present Cafe Juanita in December, he hired David Hepburn, a talented Seattle chef with ten years' experience. David arrived to manage the kitchen and do most of the cooking, although Peter to this day cooks three nights a week. the pasta is still rolled by hand on an Atlas machine each day, and one will always find a fresh, authentic Italian fish dish on the menu among other selections of lamb, veal, rabbit, and beef preparations. Fresh steamed vegetables and salad accompany all entrées, which are followed by assorted desserts and espresso. The menu appears nightly on blackboards and never includes more than eight entrées. One goal is ever-present: consistency in the quality and resentation of each dish that leaves the kitchen.

9702 NE 120th Place
Kirkland

INSALATA DI FRUTTI DI MARE

4 *pounds fresh mussels*
2 *pounds fresh steamer*
   clams
   Olive oil
1 *pound scallops, cut into*
   bite-size pieces,
   if necessary
1 *pound squid, cleaned,*
   cut into rings, and
   thoroughly dried

1½ *pounds cooked octopus*
   meat
1½ *pounds cooked bay shrimp*
   Juice of 2 lemons (more
   as needed)
2 *teaspoons Dijon-style*
   mustard
   Salt and pepper to taste
¼ *cup finely chopped*
   fresh parsley

1. Debeard the mussels and rinse well under cold running water. Rinse the clams. Coat the bottom of a large, covered frying pan or pot with the olive oil, heat over moderately high heat, and place the mussels and clams in the pan. Cover and cook over high heat just until they open. Discard any that do not open within 5 minutes.
2. Remove the mussels and clams from the frying pan. When cool enough to handle, remove the meats from the shells and place in a large mixing bowl. Reserve the pan juices, straining through damp cheesecloth if there appears to be grit in the liquid.
3. Wipe the pan dry and coat lightly again with olive oil. Quickly sauté the scallops. Remove the scallops from the pan the moment they go from translucent to opaque, 1 minute or less. Put them in the bowl with the mussels and clams.
4. With the pan still on moderately high heat, add the squid rings and sauté for 15 to 20 seconds only. Remove the squid and place in the bowl with the other cooked seafood.
5. Cut the tentacles away from the body of the octopus and slice into thin circles. Place the octopus meat in the bowl. Add the shrimp meat.

(continued next page)

6. In a smaller bowl, place the lemon juice, mustard, salt, and pepper. Gradually add ¼ cup olive oil, whisking until well-combined. Taste for tartness. Much of the lemon will be readily absorbed by the seafood, so the dressing should be rather tart. Whisk in ¼ cup of the reserved mussel and clam broth.

7. Pour the dressing over the seafood in the large mixing bowl. Add the chopped parsley. Mix well and taste again. Add more lemon, mustard, salt, and/or pepper, if desired. Let the salad marinate for a minimum of 3 to 4 hours. Serve at room temperature—not icy cold.

Note: "Green," or uncooked, shrimp in the shell can be used in place of the already-cooked bay shrimp meat. In this case, cut down the back of the shrimp with a small scissors, thus allowing for the vein removal while leaving the shell on. Dry and then sauté in the pan in the same manner as the scallops and squid, removing the shrimp the moment they turn pink. When cool enough to handle, simply pull off the shells and add the shrimp to the other ingredients.

This salad may conveniently be made a day ahead.

SPAGHETTINI WITH SMOKED SALMON

2 cups heavy cream
2 tablespoons butter
¼ pound Nova-style lox,
  finely chopped
3 ounces Parmesan cheese,
  grated
  Freshly ground black
  pepper to taste

1 tablespoon salt
1 pound fresh or dried
  spaghettini pasta
  Chopped fresh parsley
  (optional)

1. Place 5 to 6 quarts water in a large cooking pot and place, covered, over high heat. Allow to come to a full rolling boil.
2. Meanwhile, combine the cream and butter in a medium enameled skillet or saucepan. Bring to a boil and reduce until thickened enough to easily coat a spoon.
3. Add the salmon and 2 ounces of the Parmesan cheese. Stir until well mixed. Season to taste with pepper.
4. When the water comes to a boil, add the salt and, all at once, the pasta. Stir two or three times with a large pasta fork and cook until the spaghettini is softened but still slightly resistant to the bite (al dente). Fresh spaghettini will take only 2 to 3 minutes; packaged dry spaghettini will take up to 5 minutes.
5. Drain the pasta immediately in a colander; do not rinse. As soon as it is well drained, place in a warm bowl and pour on the cream/salmon mixture. Toss thoroughly and quickly. Dish the portions into heated serving bowls, top with more grated Parmesan, and serve immediately, garnished with a bit of chopped fresh parsley if desired.

PAN-BRAISED SEA BASS

1 *cup white flour*
1 *teaspoon basil*
1 *teaspoon dill weed*
1 *teaspoon thyme*
4 *(6 to 8-ounce) fillets of*
  sea bass
4 *tablespoons butter*

1 *lemon, halved,*
  seeds removed
1 *tablespoons capers,*
  rinsed and drained
Lemon wedges
Parsley sprigs

1. Combine the flour, basil, dill weed, and thyme. Dry the fillets impeccably with paper towels and dust with the seasoned flour. This can be done ahead, in which case lay the fillets side by side, not piled on each other—on a platter; cover lightly and place in the refrigerator until ready to sauté.
2. Over medium heat, melt the butter in a frying pan large enough to hold the fillets without crowding them. Put the belly side in the butter first (as this will be the presentation side on the plate) and the skin side up. (The skinned side will always have a darker color than the belly side.)
3. Cover the fillets immediately and then let braise in the butter over medium heat until the edges turn opaque. At this point, turn the fish. Squeeze with the lemon juice to taste and sprinkle the capers on and around the fish.
4. Cover again and cook for only 2 to 3 minutes, or until the fish flakes easily when a fork or knife tip is inserted into one of the muscle rings. There should be a slight line of pinkness in the very center of the fillet, as it will continue to cook for up to 1 minute after being removed from the heat.
5. Place on heated plates. Serve with lemon wedges and sprigs of parsley.

Red snapper, cod, halibut, perch, or sole can also be used.

MIXED FRESH VEGETABLES WITH PARMESAN CHEESE

6 cups fresh mixed
  vegetables of choice
Juice of ½ lemon

5 tablespoons melted butter
½ cup grated Parmesan
  cheese

1. Cut the vegetables, after having rinsed them thoroughly, into consistent sizes. If using vegetables that require slightly different cooking times, isolate them from each other so that the harder vegetables can be added to the steamer first, with the others following at appropriate intervals.
2. Place 1 inch water in the bottom of a vegetable steamer and bring the water to a boil over high heat. Place the vegetables in the steamer and, with the lid on, proceed with steaming the vegetables until they are done to your liking. Nutritional value will be retained if the vegetables are cooked to the al dente stage—slightly soft, but having a pleasant crunch.
3. Remove the vegetables from the steamer and place in a heated serving bowl. Squeeze the lemon juice over, drizzle with the melted butter, and sprinkle on the Parmesan cheese. Toss to coat the vegetables evenly and serve.

Yellow squash, zucchini, broccoli, green beans, asparagus, fennel, cauliflower, and Brussels sprouts are recommended in any combination.

CAFE JUANITA GREEN SALAD WITH HERBED VINAIGRETTE

1   *egg yolk*
    Juice of 1 lemon
2   *tablespoons white wine*
    vinegar
    Pinch of cayenne
    Pinch of salt

¾ to 1   *cup olive oil*
1 to 2   *teaspoons minced fresh*
         herbs (marjoram,
         oregano, basil, chives,
         tarragon, parsley)
2 to 3   *quarts fresh crisp greens*

1. Place the first five ingredients in a small bowl. Whisk constantly while adding the olive oil to taste. (Less oil will produce a more vinegary taste.) Whisk in the minced herbs.
2. Rinse the greens thoroughly and dry with paper towels or in a salad spinner. Tear into salad pieces.
3. Drizzle the dressing over the greens and toss to thoroughly coat each leaf.

Note: Any combination of herbs will work, depending on your preferences. In the winter all you will find—unless you maintain your own herbs—is parsley; I prefer that alone to using dried herbs.

If the leaves of greens are not thoroughly dry, the dressing will not adhere properly to the surfaces, resulting in a flavorless salad with all the dressing sitting in a puddle at the bottom of the bowl.

SPUMA DI CIOCCOLATA

4 ounces sweet chocolate
  or 3 ounces semi-sweet
  chocolate and 1 ounce
  butter)
2 tablespoons brewed
  espresso or strong coffee

¼ cup dark rum
¼ cup sugar
4 eggs, separated
2 cups heavy cream
  Shaved chocolate

1. Melt the chocolate with the coffee in a small pan that is sitting over boiling water. Stir until smooth; set aside.
2. Make a syrup of the rum and sugar by mixing them together in a small saucepan and boiling the mixture for 1 minute.
3. After letting the syrup cool for a few moments, whisk it into the egg yolks in a medium-size bowl, beating until thick.
4. Add the melted chocolate to the egg yolk mixture.
5. In a separate, clean bowl, beat the egg whites until stiff. Fold into the chocolate mixture. Allow the mixture to cool.
6. In another clean bowl, beat the cream until stiff and fold it into the chocolate mixture. Make sure the cream and chocolate are well blended.
7. Place the Spuma di Cioccolata in sherbet or parfait glasses and top with shaved chocolate. Chill until ready to serve.

Dinner for Six

Baby Shrimp in Belgian Endive

Chilled Avocado Soup with Fresh Basil

Pasta della Casa con Prosciutto

Roman-Style Roast Leg of Lamb with Sautéed Spinach

Fresh Fruit with Raspberry Bordeaux and Crème Fraîche

Wine:

With the Lamb—Rutherford Hill Chardonnnay or Pinot Noir

With the Dessert—Robertson's Tawny Port

Collins Jones, Owner & Chef

CAFE SABIKA

For eight out of the eleven years that Cafe Sabika has existed, Collins Jones has been the sole owner and chef. Jones has steadfastly reigned over his restaurant from the open kitchen. He still works in full view of his customers, carefully preparing each meal that has been ordered. He moves quickly and expertly. Everything is at his fingertips: copper pots and pans hang overhead, a wine rack is mounted on the wall nearby, the tomatoes, lemons and avocados are in a large wire basket sitting on the counter near an old copper coffee urn. Many antique kitchen accessories add charm to his domain. "With the kitchen open, I have a chance to communicate with my customers, and I like that."

Collins Jones feels that the most unique thing about Cafe Sabika is the atmosphere: "People seem to find it very relaxing here. They feel at home." A small, unpretentious, cozy restaurant, the Cafe seats only thirty-five at the sometimes square, sometimes round, sometimes oval, but always very old tables surrounded by equally varied antique wooden chairs. The twenty-five-year-old fern in the window has become a tradition, as has the cafe itself.

"Eleven years ago," explains Jones, "Cafe Sabika pioneered the idea of a restaurant doing a daily market shopping. I have stuck with the philosophy of using fresh, natural ingredients as much as possible. Each morning I start my day in the Pike Place Market where I buy meat, seafood, produce, and cheese." The cafe's menu is not large; it features pasta, chicken, and seafood, and it changes every two weeks. Dinners are prepared in the Mediterranean style, with the emphasis on Spanish, French, and Italian cuisines.

Cafe Sabika is unique mostly because Collins Jones is unique. "The recipes I use are pretty much out of my head. Basically, I use a classic approach—Julia Child is my favorite—but then I invent my own versions of recipes. Coming up with new ideas is a creative outlet for me," and, according to his customers, an innovative and delicious experience in fine cuisine.

315 East Pine

CAFE SABIKA

BABY SHRIMP IN BELGIAN ENDIVE

1 pound Belgian endive	3 tablespoons mayonnaise
1 pound baby shrimp	Fresh dill sprigs
1 teaspoon chopped fresh	1 lemon, sliced
dill weed	

1. Arrange the endive leaves on a chilled platter and cover with plastic wrap. Refrigerate until ready to serve.
2. When ready to serve, mix the shrimp, dill, and mayonnaise. Spoon this mixture onto the endive leaves.
3. Garnish with sprigs of fresh dill and lemon slices.

CHILLED AVOCADO SOUP
with Fresh Basil

4 ripe avocados	3 stalks celery, chopped
1 quart chicken consommé	1 bunch fresh basil, chopped
Tabasco sauce	1 large tomato, peeled
Juice of 1 lemon	and chopped
1 small red onion, chopped	Juice of 1 lime

1. Place 2 avocados, 2 cups chicken consommé, a dash of Tabasco, the juice of ½ lemon and ½ cup water in a blender. Process until creamy. Pour into a storage jar. Repeat this process and combine with the first batch.
2. Add the chopped red onion, celery, basil, tomato, and lime juice. Stir well to blend.
3. Chill for several hours before serving.

This recipe may be prepared well in advance of serving. I think the combination of lime and basil is exceptional in flavor. If you don't wish to make your own consommé, Linden's canned clear chicken broth is acceptable.

PASTA DELLA CASA CON PROSCIUTTO

½ *pound snow peas*
3 *carrots*
1 *small zucchini*
3 *scallions, whites only*
½ *pound mushrooms*
2 *pounds fresh fettuccini*
2 *tablespoons olive oil*

1 *clove garlic, pressed*
Salt
Freshly ground pepper
¼ *pound prosciutto, finely diced*
½ *pound Italian Parmesan cheese, grated*

1. Prepare all vegetables ahead of time: clean the snow peas, thinly slice the carrots and steam al dente, slice the zucchini, slice in julienne the whites of the scallions, and slice the mushrooms. Put all of the prepared vegetables into a salad bowl, toss, and keep in the refrigerator until ready to serve.
2. When ready to serve, put the fettuccini into boiling water. For fresh pasta, cook for 3 minutes only.
3. While the pasta is cooking, quickly sauté the vegetables in the olive oil, adding the garlic and salt and pepper to taste.
4. Drain the pasta and immediately pour the cooked vegetables over. Add the prosciutto, grated Parmesan, and several grinds of pepper. Toss and serve.

ROMAN-STYLE ROAST LEG OF LAMB

1 *tablespoon juniper berries*
3 *cloves garlic, pressed*
1 *teaspoon rosemary*
1 *teaspoon oregano*
 Freshly ground pepper
1 *(7-pound) leg of lamb,*
 boned

Olive oil
Pinch of salt
1 *cup dry white wine*
 SAUTÉED SPINACH
 (see next page)

1. Preheat oven to 425°.
2. Crush the juniper berries with a mortar and pestle. Add the garlic, rosemary, oregano, and pepper, mixing into a paste.
3. Place the seasoning inside the cavity of the boned lamb leg. Truss and rub the leg with olive oil, salt, and ground pepper.
4. Place the roast on a rack in a shallow pan. Roast in preheated oven for 25 minutes. Open the oven door for about 2 minutes and let the oven cool to 350°. Roast for another 1 to 1½ hours, basting with white wine every 30 minutes. (In one additional hour, the lamb should be medium rare. For well done, another hour of cooking time may be needed.)
5. Remove the roast from the rack. Strain the juices and set aside. The lamb may be kept warm in the oven until ready to serve.
6. Place the leg of lamb on a platter, placing the Sautéed Spinach around the sides. Serve with the reserved pan juices.

This is an authentic Roman recipe which I learned from a family I lived with in San Francisco.

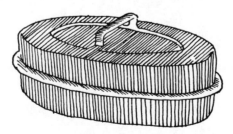

SAUTÉED SPINACH

4 bunches fresh spinach
4 tablespoons butter
¼ cup olive oil

2 cloves garlic, pressed
Salt and pepper
Juice of 2 lemons

1. Wash the spinach thoroughly. Drain briefly and place in a pot; steam 1 minute in the water remaining on the leaves.
2. Squeeze the spinach into several small balls. Chop finely.
3. Heat the butter and olive oil in a sauté pan over high heat. Add the garlic, salt, pepper, lemon juice, and chopped spinach and sauté until heated through and the flavors are blended.

CAFE SABIKA

FRESH FRUIT WITH RASPBERRY BORDEAUX AND CRÈME FRAÎCHE

4 ripe peaches
2 pints raspberries
1 pint strawberries,
   cleaned and sliced

½ cup Raspberry Bordeaux
   (French raspberry
   liqueur)
CRÈME FRAÎCHE

1. Slice the peaches. Layer in a medium-sized glass serving bowl. Top with the raspberries, and, finally, with sliced strawberries.
2. Cover with the Raspberry Bordeaux. Chill until ready to serve.
3. At serving time, spoon into individual bowls and pass the Crème Fraîche to be poured over the fruit.

CRÈME FRAÎCHE

2 tablespoons buttermilk

1 quart heavy cream

Add the buttermilk to the cream. Let stand at room temperature for 12 hours.

This dessert is delicious, simple, and refreshing after a big meal.

Les Copains

Dinner for Six

Fresh Crayfish with Green Herbal Mayonnaise

Savory Marrow Custards with Rhubarb Sauce

Apple-Sage Ice

Roast Rack of Lamb with Beets and Pears

Bibb Salad with Butter-Shallot Dressing

Gooseberry Fool

Wine:

*With the Crayfish and the Marrow Custards—Philipponnat
Champagne Blanc de Blancs, Brut, Cuvée Première, 1976*

With the Lamb—Barolo, Brunate Marcarini, 1971

*With the Gooseberry Fool—Hinzerling Gewürztraminer,
Select Cluster Late Harvest, 1979*

*Bruce Naftaly, William Knospe, Marguerite Margason, Art Harris,
Sally Harris, & Josh Keeler, Owners*

LES COPAINS

Les Copains is derived from the Latin *cum panis*, meaning "with bread." Combined with the French *copain*, meaning "pal" or "chum," the essence of this unique Wallingford restaurant emerges: people and friends coming together to break bread and share good feelings. Les Copain's six owners steadfastly agree that their restaurant must serve fresh, local and seasonal food; also, that ingredients be carefully selected and prepared to please and excite, and that food be served with home-like conviviality by waiters sensitive to individual tastes.

In keeping with this emphasis on neighborliness, Les Copains encourages customers to use the restaurant as a friendly meeting place. The invitation is readily and frequently accepted. Guests gather for conversation and coffee, debates over espresso and wines by the glass, and before and after-theater rendezvous over fruit and cheese or the much-acclaimed charcuterie plates, in addition to the regular lunch and dinner trade.

The charcuterie, a unique feature of the restaurant and the brainchild of co-owner Marguerite Margason, was designed to provide both a tasty in-house assortment of pâtés, sausages, and salads and a take-out service for customers wishing to enjoy the viands at home. As in the restaurant, all the mayonnaise, mustards, and condiments at the charcuterie are freshly prepared. If they wish, customers may also purchase wines and the luscious baked goods furnished by the Boulangerie next door.

Head chef Bruce Naftaly creates most dishes, using French techniques. Yet, what is presented assumes a regional flavor, since ingredients are supplied primarily by local purveyors. Indeed, the owners of Les Copains make a point of supporting the local merchants. Often, their insistence on freshness, superiority, and the unusual has influenced the appearance of new products on the market.

The rich, homey atmosphere is effected by the presence of Chinese hand-crocheted lace placemats, soft green carpets, work by local artists on the off-white walls, and deep-stained wood tables. Indirect lighting overhead glows warmly over the amiable chatter and enjoyable eating that happily goes on.

2202 North 45th

FRESH CRAYFISH

2 cups dry white wine
2 cups Fish Fumet (see
   index) or good stock
   (optional)
   Several sprigs fresh parsley
6 to 8 sprigs fresh tarragon
1 dried hot red pepper
½ teaspoon whole
   peppercorns
1 whole allspice berry

½ onion, sliced in rings
   or coarsely chopped
   Several lovage leaves
24 live crayfish
   GREEN HERBAL
   MAYONNAISE
   (see next page)
   Fennel greens
   Pansies or other edible
   flowers

1. Combine all ingredients except a few of the lovage leaves, the crayfish, mayonnaise, fennel, and flowers in a large stock pot. Add 4 quarts water and bring slowly to a boil. Cover and simmer for 30 minutes.
2. Rinse the crayfish. Place one at a time on the edge of a counter so that the tail overhangs slightly, holding firmly with a towel to avoid being pinched. Lift the middle tail shell flange and twist sharply. Gently pull away from the body; a blackish ribbon should come away, attached to the flange. Remove and discard this ribbon.
3. Uncover the simmering bouillon and return to a full boil. Plunge six or eight crayfish at a time into the bouillon. They will quickly turn from their blackish color to a bright red. Cook approximately 4 minutes and remove to a platter to cool. Repeat for remaining crayfish.
4. Strain 2 cups of the poaching bouillon into a saucepan over high heat. Reduce to about 2 tablespoons.
5. Cool the bouillon reduction to room temperature and beat into the mayonnaise. Taste the mayonnaise and correct seasoning if necessary. Refrigerate.
6. To serve, arrange four crayfish on each plate. Place a good dab of mayonnaise in the center and garnish with the reserved lovage, fennel greens, and edible flowers.

If you are unable to locate the greens suggested in the recipe, experiment with greens that are readily available, such as basil or watercress.

LES COPAINS

GREEN HERBAL MAYONNAISE

4 egg yolks
1 cup olive oil
1 cup peanut oil
2 tablespoons red wine
   vinegar, plus more
   to taste
Salt

Freshly ground white
   pepper
½ bunch fresh sorrel
½ bunch lamb's quarter
¼ bunch lovage
¼ bunch fennel greens

1. Whisk the egg yolks in a bowl until thick and lemon colored. Reserving 1 tablespoon oil, begin adding the oils, separately or combined, drop by drop at first. As the emulsion thickens, gradually add the oils faster. If the addition is rushed, the emulsion may break—take a fresh yolk and a clean bowl and, a little more gradually, whisk in the broken mixture and the remainder of the oil.
2. Season to taste with salt and white pepper. Taste again and add more vinegar if desired. Set aside.
3. Purée the greens with the reserved 1 tablespoon oil until smooth. (Use a food processor fitted with a steel blade, if available; otherwise, pound to a paste with a mortar and pestle and pass through a sieve.) Taste and correct the proportions of the greens to taste.
4. Slowly beat the purée of greens into the mayonnaise.

If the sorrel provides insufficient tartness, add a little red wine vinegar. Mayonnaise is very forgiving: it may be thickened with more oil, or combined with more mayonnaise if oversalted or made with too much vinegar. Heavy cream may be added if it is too thick.

LES COPAINS

SAVORY MARROW CUSTARDS

7 ounces beef marrow,
   at room temperature
1 cup milk, warmed
⅔ cup strong beef
   demi-glace, warmed
1½ teaspoons salt

¼ teaspoon white pepper
½ teaspoon ground bay leaf
¼ teaspoon ground sage
3 whole eggs
5 egg yolks
   RHUBARB SAUCE

1. Preheat oven to 275°.
2. Place the marrow, milk, and beef demi-glace in the bowl of a food processor fitted with a steel blade and blend for several minutes. If the mixture refuses to form a smooth emulsion, pour it into a saucepan, heat over moderate flame, and whisk until liquefied; remove from heat and cool slightly.
3. Add the seasonings and whisk in the whole eggs and egg yolks.
4. Pour into six buttered ramekins. Select a pan large enough to hold all the ramekins, add water to come halfway up the containers, and bake in preheated oven for 40 minutes or until a sharp knife inserted into the custard comes out clean. Cool, cover, and refrigerate.
5. Bring the sauce to room temperature, so as to liquefy the jelly.
6. Carefully slide a small, sharp knife arund the side of each custard ramekin and invert onto individual plates. Spoon some of the sauce over each, so that the custard appears to be floating in a pool of sauce. Pass the rest of the sauce in a separate bowl or sauceboat.

Some butchers will remove the bone marrow for you, if given advance notice.

RHUBARB SAUCE

1½ cups beef demi-glace
1½ cups Pinot Noir
   grape must (juice)
2 cups sliced rhubarb,
   in 2-inch pieces

½ cup lightly packed
   lovage leaves
2 tablespoons dried whole
   sage, or ½ bunch
   fresh

Place all ingredients in a saucepan and simmer for 45 minutes to 1 hour over low heat. Strain and cool.

APPLE-SAGE ICE

6 cups fresh apple cider
2 green apples (Golden
    Criterion variety are
    best), peeled, cored,
    and cut into small pieces

½ bunch sage, tied in
    cheesecloth, plus 6 leaves
6 rose petals (optional)

1. In a stainless steel or enameled saucepan, combine the cider, apples, and ½ bunch sage. Cook slowly over moderately low heat until the liquid is reduced by one-third and the apples are very soft.
2. Remove the sage. Strain the liquid through a fine sieve and set aside.
3. Thoroughly purée the apples which have been trapped in the strainer in a food mill or processor.
4. Return the apple purée to the liquid and mix thoroughly. Place the mixture in a shallow pan and place in the freezer. Stir every 15 minutes until frozen to assure an even texture.
5. To serve, scrape the golden crystals of ice into chilled wine glasses. Garnish each with a sage leaf and, perhaps, a rose petal.

A palate-clearing ice created by Chef Naftaly, this cool concoction truly provides a refreshing, unusual break between courses.

ROAST RACK OF LAMB WITH BEETS AND PEARS

⅓ pound beets (any size,
    peeled, trimmed, and
    washed
6 pears (preferably Bosc)
6 cloves garlic, peeled
    DARK LAMB STOCK
    (see p. 60)
18 baby beets, no larger
    than golf balls

3 racks of lamb, trimmed
1 cup dry red wine
¾ tablespoon salt, or to taste
½ teaspoon freshly ground
    pepper, or to taste
1 teaspoon poire (French
    pear brandy—optional)
6 nasturtium blossoms

1. Preheat oven to 500°.
2. Cut the ⅓ pound beets into small pieces. Peel and core 3 pears and cut into pieces of a similar size.
3. Combine the cut beets and pears, garlic, and all but 2 cups of the lamb stock in a stainless steel or enameled saucepan. Cook slowly, uncovered, until the liquid has been reduced by half—2 to 3 hours.
4. Core the remaining 3 pears and cut each in sixths. Trim and scrub the baby beets.
5. Over moderately high heat, sear the lamb racks on all sides in a roasting pan with a little oil. Add the pear sections and baby beets, taking care to place the pears either on the lamb or on the beets to prevent burning. Place the roasting pan in the preheated oven and roast until medium-rare, about 20 minutes.
6. Remove the lamb, beets, and pears from the pan. Pour off the fat, place the pan over high heat, and deglaze with the red wine. Strain the liquid into the sauce. Cover the lamb and vegetables with foil while finishing the sauce.
7. When the sauce has been properly reduced, purée in a food processor or mill. Strain the purée through a sturdy strainer into the same saucepan, pressing the strained matter to extract all the juices. The purée should be very smooth, yet easily able to coat a spoon. If too thick, thin with some or all of the reserved stock; if too thin, reduce further over moderate heat, stirring constantly.
8. Taste for seasoning, adding salt and pepper as desired. Add the poire if desired to bring out the flavor of the pears.
9. Ladle the sauce onto warmed plates to cover. Cut the lamb racks into individual chops and arrange over the sauce, four to a plate, in a pinwheel design. Arrange three baby beets and three roasted pear sections on each plate. Garnish each with a well-placed nasturtium and serve.

Salt will bring out the flavor of the lamb in the sauce; the amount needed may be surprising—perhaps as much as 1 tablespoon.

LES COPAINS

DARK LAMB STOCK

¼ cup olive or vegetable oil

4 pounds lamb scraps and
   bones, cut into small
   pieces

4 onions, peeled and cut
   in small pieces

4 carrots, washed, trimmed,
   and cut in small pieces

8 stalks celery, washed and
   cut in small pieces

1½ quarts dry red wine

1 quart Madeira

4 bay leaves

4 sprigs fresh thyme

4 sprigs fresh rosemary

4 sprigs fresh parsley,
   stems included

4 cloves garlic

1. In a stock pot large enough to hold all the ingredients, heat the oil until almost smoking. Add half the lamb scraps and bones and brown, turning and scraping the bottom of the pan, for 10 to 15 minutes or until the meat is well browned.
2. Add half the vegetables and repeat the same process to brown.
3. When all is well browned, add half the red wine and Madeira to deglaze the pan, stirring and scraping constantly. Reduce the liquid to a very small volume which is almost as thick as a syrup.
4. Add cold water just to cover. Add half the herbs and slowly bring to a boil. Simmer, half-covered, for at least 4 hours—the minimum required to extract the flavor from the ingredients; cook longer if time permits. Scum which accumulates on the surface should be skimmed regularly, and the water level should be maintained to barely cover.
5. Strain the liquid. Skim the fat, or refrigerate to congeal it and remove.
6. Repeat the process with the remaining half of the ingredients; however, when the time comes to add water, instead add the stock just made.

The secret of a wonderful, intensely flavored sauce is a well-made stock. This stock is twice as flavorful as one made with water alone, and when used as the basis for the sauce, yields an intense, rich, delicious flavor. This recipe, though somewhat elaborate, is actually quite a condensation from what is done at Les Copains.

BIBB SALAD WITH BUTTER-SHALLOT DRESSING

½ pound unsalted butter
2 small shallots, peeled
  and finely chopped
  Red wine vinegar

3 small heads Bibb or butter
  lettuce, washed and dried
  Rose petals (optional)

1. Melt the butter over low heat, being careful not to let it come anywhere near boiling. Carefully skim off the residue that forms on top, then spoon or very carefully pour off into a clean pan the clear, yellow liquid, stopping when you come to the milky substance resting at the bottom of the pan.
2. To the clarified butter in the clean pan, add the chopped shallots and a little red wine vinegar—start with 1 teaspoon. Heat until hot to touch but, again, nowhere near the boil. Stir well with a ladle and taste. Add a little more vinegar if you like. Keep warm until ready to serve.
3. Stir the dressing well and toss with the lettuce in a warm bowl. Place the salad on warm serving plates and garnish with rose petals if desired. Serve immediately or the dressing will congeal.

GOOSEBERRY FOOL

¾ to 1 pound gooseberries,
  rinsed and drained
4 to 6 tablespoons unsalted
  butter

Superfine sugar to taste
1 to 1½ cups heavy cream,
  whipped
  Violas (garnish—optional)

1. Top and tail the gooseberries with a pair of scissors. Stew in the butter in a covered stainless steel or enameled pan over low heat until yellow and lightly cooked.
2. Lightly crush the berries with a fork. Taste and, according to the tartness of the fruit, sweeten with superfine sugar as desired. Allow to cool.
3. Fold the berry purée into the whipped cream. Serve in chilled glasses, garnished with violas or any other delicacy of choice.
   The cream will hold from 2 to 4 hours under refrigeration, but will collapse if made too far ahead or if kept too warm. One option is to have the berries cooked, crushed, and cooled (and have the serving dishes in the refrigerator, too), and simply whip the cream after dinner, fold in the berries, and dish into the cold glasses.

COSTAS OPA

Dinner for Six

Saganaki

Horiatiki Salad

Greek Beef Souvlaki

Rice Pilaf

Tzatziki

Galaktoboureko

Wine:

With the Saganaki and/or Salad—Kokineli,
or
Retsina,
or
Santa Laura

With the Souvlaki—red Demestica or Sanielis

Costas Antonopoulos, Owner & Chef

COSTAS OPA

A peculiar homesickness can beset travelers returned from Greece. Thoughts of the coastline, the laughter, dancing, and noshing in tavernas, the flaky, buttery pastries, the aromatic souvlaki stands, the fresh salads and feta in olive oil and vinegar, the creamy, herb-imbued casseroles—all urge a longing to catch the earliest plane to Athens. Aware that these images have become vital to memories, and nostalgic himself, Costas Antonopoulos created the next best thing to being there: Costas Opa.

Costas Opa, which crosses a Greek taverna with a formal restaurant, makes reminiscing a pleasure. Tantalizing odors accost the entering guest, and one can see food displayed behind glass dividers. Greek music, Greek fabrics and rugs, pottery, white stucco, and hanging copper enhance the mood and complete the setting.

Yet, Costas's primary concern is not to offer an ersatz return; it is, instead, to serve authentic Greek food and classic Greek wines. One may recall warm evenings on a terrace, sipping retsina and leisurely scooping up taramosalata, melizanosalata, hummos and tzatziki with warm pita bread. The traditional saganaki cheese appetizer flamed at the table is a favorite. And if not too filled with feta cheese, olives, and peppers, one can take on the entrées with gusto: dolmades, gyros, moussaka, kalamari, spanakopita, roast lamb, herbed chicken, paidakia, or bakaliaros skordalia, which is cod dipped in egg batter and pan-fried with a pungent garlic sauce.

Costas still does much of the cooking and spends hours in the kitchen supervising the quality of prepared dishes. He came to the United States in 1968 after spending a year in Vancouver, B.C., and since has worked exclusively in the restaurant business. He was one of the original partners of the Continental Pastry Shop on University Avenue, then established two other restaurants before opening Costas Opa in 1981.

3400 Fremont North

SAGANAKI

18 ounces Kafalotyri or
Pecorino Romano cheese
3 large eggs, lightly beaten
Flour
3 to 4 tablespoons olive oil

1½ tablespoons Metaxa brandy
Lemon wedges
Chopped fresh parsley
Pita or any crusty bread

1. In a warm oven, preheat a serving dish that is able to withstand and retain heat. It must get warm enough to heat the brandy for flambéing.
2. Slice the cheese into even pieces ¼ inch thick, preferably triangles or squares. Dip into the beaten eggs and dredge in flour to coat well.
3. Heat the olive oil over medium heat in a heavy-bottomed skillet large enough to hold all the cheese. When hot, place the coated cheese pieces in the pan and fry on one side until golden brown.
4. Turn with a spatula and fry about 1 minute. Transfer, browned side up, to the heated serving dish. Take immediately to the table.
5. Pour the brandy over and, keeping the dish away from your hair, ignite with a match. At this point it is important to shout "Opa!" very loudly.
6. When the flames die out, squeeze 1 or 2 lemon wedges over the cheese. Garnish with the chopped parsley and remaining lemon wedges and serve with pita or other bread.

HORIATIKI SALAD

6 tomatoes
3 cucumbers
1 onion
1 green bell pepper
½ pound feta cheese
¾ cup olive oil
   (approximately)

¼ cup red wine vinegar
   (approximately)
Salt and freshly ground
   black pepper
12 peperoncini (optional)
18 to 24 Greek olives

1. Dice the tomatoes in ½-inch cubes. Peel and dice the cucumbers in ½-inch cubes. Place in a large salad bowl.
2. Slice the onion and bell pepper into 12 thin rings each; quarter the rings and add to the salad.
3. Slice the feta cheese about ¼ inch thick. Crumble over the salad.
4. Sprinkle the olive oil over, followed by the vinegar or to taste. Salt lightly and grind fresh pepper over. Toss until well coated. coated.
5. Taste for seasoning. Add more vinegar if tartness is lacking; add more oil if too tart. Divide among six plates or bowls. Garnish with the peperoncini, if desired, and the olives.

This salad is most superb when made with vine-ripened tomatoes, garden cucumbers, and sweet, tender onions. In any case, be sure to select firm but ripe tomatoes for the best result.

GREEK BEEF SOUVLAKI

2 *pounds beef sirloin tip*
  or tenderloin
4 *large cloves garlic, minced*
½ *cup olive oil*
¼ *cup dry white wine*
⅛ *teaspoon black pepper*
1 *tablespoon Greek oregano*
1 *large onion, cut in*
  eighths and separated

1 *bell pepper, cut*
  in 1" squares
Salt to taste
Parsley sprigs
Lemon wedges
Cherry tomatoes

1. Remove all the fat and connective tissue from the meat. Cut in 1-inch cubes and place in a bowl large enough to hold it with enough room to gently toss in the marinade.
2. Add the garlic, olive oil, white wine, pepper, and oregano. Toss to coat the meat evenly and thoroughly. The onion and pepper may, optionally, be marinated with the meat. Store the mixture overnight, well covered, in the refrigerator.
3. Skewer the meat with the onion and pepper, 1 piece of onion between each piece of meat, with perhaps only 1 or 2 pieces of pepper on each skewer. Reserve the marinade for basting. Lay the skewers on a plate, cover, and return to the refrigerator.
4. Remove the skewers from the refrigerator about 15 minutes before serving time. Preheat grill, broiler, or frying pan. If using the broiler, place the skewers on a cookie sheet or pan large enough to hold without crowding. If using a frying pan, preheat over moderately high heat. Cook, turning twice and salting and basting with the reserved marinade each time, for 7 to 12 minutes or until done to taste.
5. Remove to a heated platter. Garnish with parsley, lemon wedges, and cherry tomatoes. Serve with Rice Pilaf and Tzatziki.

One of the keys to tender, succulent souvlaki—in addition to the quality of meat used—is to not salt the meat until it is cooking.

RICE PILAF

¼ cup olive oil
1 small onion, diced small
1 cup long-grain rice
2 cups hot Chicken Stock
  (see index), canned
  chicken broth, or bouillon

⅛ teaspoon salt
  (approximately)
2 tablespoons butter

1. Heat the olive oil in a heavy-bottomed skillet over moderately high heat. Add the onion and cook for 4 to 5 minutes, or until softened and lightly browned.
2. Add the rice and cook, stirring constantly, for 3 minutes; towards the end of this time you should hear a crackling sound.
3. Add the hot stock, salt, and butter. If the stock is not very salty, you may wish to add more salt. Stir once or twice. Place the lid on the pan as soon as the liquid comes to a boil. Reduce heat to low and cook for 15 to 20 minutes, testing at 15 minutes to see if all the liquid has been absorbed and the grains are separated and sufficiently cooked.
4. Stir gently and remove to a heated serving dish.

As a result of the rice absorbing the oil in step 2, the grains become fluffy and well separated when steamed. This rice is equally delicious with grilled, broiled, or baked meat, fish or poultry.

TZATZIKI

4 large cloves garlic
  Pinch of salt
½ to 1 whole cucumber,
  washed and dried

1 quart plain yogurt
¼ cup olive oil
¼ cup red wine vinegar

1. Mash the garlic cloves with the flat of a large knife or cleaver. Add the salt and continue to mash until a fine paste is formed.

2. Grate the unpeeled cucumber. Combine in a bowl with the yogurt, mashed garlic, oil, and vinegar. Mix thoroughly. Taste; if there is no pronounced garlic flavor, mash and add more.
3. Let sit for several hours at room temperature or overnight in the refrigerator.

This is a typical Greek hors d'oeuvre. It is also delicious, however, as an accompaniment to lamb or beef.

GALAKTOBOUREKO

1 *pound fillo leaves,*
  at room temperature
½ *pound butter, melted*
  CUSTARD (see p. 71)

SYRUP (see p. 71)
Cinnamon (optional)
Sliced orange (optional)

Method 1 (Pan-Style):

1. Preheat oven to 350°.
2. Layer 4 sheets of fillo, each lightly but completely buttered, on one side in a loaf pan in such a way that enough of an overhang is left all the way around to fold over the top of the Custard. Be sure that the leaves overlap adequately to seal the Custard within them.
3. Spread the Custard evenly within the fillo leaves. Fold the overhanging leaves to cover.
4. Layer 3 to 5 more lightly but evenly buttered fillo leaves over. Top with an unbuttered leaf. Fold the edges and corners neatly.
5. With a sharp knife, cut diagonally through only the two top layers of fillo to mark diamond-shaped portions. Butter the top layer of fillo.
6. Bake in preheated oven for approximately 45 minutes, or until the fillo is puffed and golden brown. (Begin checking at 30 minutes if you suspect your oven to operate hot.) Remove and pour the cooled Syrup over the surface. Allow to cool for at least 1 hour or until set before cutting into portions.

If using this traditional method of preparation, the custard may be slightly warm to start. *(continued next page)*

Method 2 (Floyeres):

1. Preheat oven to 350°.
2. Layer 2 fillo leaves, each lightly but evenly buttered on one side, on a working surface. Center ½ cup (or an ice-cream scoop) of the Custard on the nearest end of the top leaf. Fold both sides of the fillo toward the center, partially covering the custard. Starting at the end with the custard, roll up like an egg roll. Place seam side down in a deep pan. Butter the top and ends.
3. Repeat until all the Custard is used, placing 1 inch apart in the pan.
4. Bake in preheated oven for 30 minutes or until puffed and golden brown, beginning to check at 20 minutes. Remove from the oven and pour the cooled Syrup over. Serve immediately or allow to cool; pour additional syrup from the pan over the rolls at serving time. Lightly sprinkle with cinnamon and top each with a thin slice of orange.

To manage the rolling of the Floyeres, or flutes, you must be sure the custard is thoroughly cooled and thickened beforehand. The name for this method of preparation derives from the similarity to the reed flutes of the Greek shepherds.

COSTAS OPA

CUSTARD

6 cups whole milk
1⅔ cups sugar
½ cup plus 1 tablespoon
  cream of wheat

5 eggs
  Peel of ½ lemon, finely
  grated
1 teaspoon vanilla extract

1. Place the milk and half the sugar in a saucepan. Bring to a boil, stirring frequently.
2. In a mixing bowl large enough to hold all the ingredients, place the remaining sugar, the cream of wheat, and eggs. Whisk for 2 to 3 minutes.
3. As soon as the milk reaches a boil, whisk gradually into the egg mixture, stirring constantly. Continue to stir—vigorously at first, more slowly toward the end, and being sure to reach to the bottom of the bowl—until all ingredients are well combined.
4. Add the grated lemon peel and vanilla extract and continue to whisk for 3 to 4 minutes. The mixture will begin to thicken slightly, and barely begin to bubble, around the edges. At this point, stop beating—it will curdle if overbeaten. Allow to cool before using.

It is ideal to make the custard in the morning, or even the day ahead, especially if using the second method of preparation.

SYRUP

2 cups sugar
  Juice of 1 lemon

1 stick cinnamon

Place the ingredients with 1 cup water in a small saucepan. Bring to a boil and cook for 1 minute. Remove from heat and allow to cool.

Dinner for Four

French Onion Soup

Shrimp and Butter Lettuce Salad

Stir-Fry Vegetables and Prawns

Herbed and Wild Rice

Chocolate Mousse Pie

Wine:

Puligny-Montrachet

Bill & John Schwartz, Owners
Al Culdice, Manager
Michael Schwartz, Assistant Manager
Michael Cowart, Chef

DANIEL'S BROILER

V ivid, multi-colored sails on boats almost near enough to touch, a breathtaking view of Mount Rainier on a clear night, and the joy of watching a full moon rise over Bellevue: all this and more comes with the dinner at Daniel's Broiler. From every seat in the dining room, one can observe the majesty of Lake Washington, for Daniel's Broiler virtually sits on the shores of the lake, and many of the dinner patrons arrive by boat. The setting is the YABA Yacht Basin at Leschi, in the space that once housed the picturesque Seaborn's Marina. Now the floor-to-ceiling wood-frame windows, designed in a stunning geometric pattern, enclose the elegant, comfortable, contemporary retreat where dinner is served nightly.

The restaurant first opened in January 1980, but its owner Dan Sandal sold it a year later to the Butcher Organization, an association of restaurants headed by the Schwartz brothers, Bill and John. The organization embraces Henry's Off Broadway, Benjamin's, two Butcher restaurants, and five Sandwich Shop and Pie Places. Daniel's is the smallest of the dinner restaurants and a unique complement to its siblings. Michael Schwartz, brother of Bill and John and manager of Daniel's, explains. "We are more than a steak house: we have become a specialized broiler. Our emphasis now is on seafood because our customers have dictated their preference. Probably seventy to eighty percent of the dinners we serve are seafood, and most are broiled right in full view of the customer."

"We serve fairly simple food," adds the chef, Michael Cowart, "but we use the best ingredients possible." The patron's wishes are considered foremost. "We are a customer-oriented restaurant; if someone requests a special sauce or a certain seasoning, and we have the ingredients in our kitchen, we will prepare it gladly."

From the ninety-six candle-like lights on the extraordinary copper chandelier which encompasses the entire ceiling of the restaurant, to the constantly changing view from the windows, Daniel's Broiler is a comfortably elegant, predictably delicious place to dine.

200 Lake Washington Boulevard

DANIEL'S BROILER

FRENCH ONION SOUP

4 tablespoons butter
4 onions, cut in ¼"
   julienne
2 cloves garlic, minced
¼ cup flour
5⅓ cups BROWN STOCK
   (see next page) or
   beef broth
⅓ cup Chablis
¼ teaspoon coarsely ground
   pepper

3 tablespoons olive oil
   (approximately)
8 thin slices French
   baguette loaf
½ pound Gruyère cheese,
   shredded
2 teaspoons chopped fresh
   parsley

1. Preheat oven to 350°.
2. Melt the butter in a sauté pan over medium-high heat. Add the onions and 1 minced clove of garlic; sauté until the onions are lightly browned.
3. Spread the flour over the surface of a baking pan and bake in pre-heated oven until lightly browned. Add to the onions and mix well.
4. Place the Brown Stock in a large pot. Stir in the onion mixture, wine, and pepper. Bring to a boil, reduce heat, and simmer 1 hour, skimming the surface every 15 minutes.
5. Sauté the remaining garlic in about 3 tablespoons olive oil until it begins to brown. Remove the garlic and discard; brown the sliced bread well in the seasoned oil.
6. A few minutes before serving, preheat the broiler. Ladle the soup into individual heated crocks. Top each serving with two of the croutons and one-fourth of the shredded cheese. Place under the broiler until the cheese is melted and very lightly browned. Garnish each with a sprinkle of chopped parsley and serve.

BROWN STOCK

2½ pounds beef or veal bones
    or trimmings (or a
    combination)
½ onion, diced large
1 stalk celery, diced large
1 carrot, sliced in large
    chunks
1 bay leaf

1 clove garlic, halved
    Pinch of thyme
1 cup red wine
1 cup white wine
3 to 4 whole peppercorns
    Salt

1. Break the bones with a heavy cleaver. Place the bones and trimmings in a roasting pan and bake at 300° for 1 hour or until the bones are well browned.
2. Add the vegetables, bay leaf, and garlic. Bake until all are tender, about 30 minutes.
3. Add the thyme and red and white wines; deglaze the pan over high heat. Transfer everything to a large stock pot.
4. Add 3 quarts water and the peppercorns and bring to a boil. Cook until reduced by half, skimming frequently.
5. Strain through a china cap, discarding all solid matter. Return to heat, skimming until clear.
6. Pass through a fine-mesh sieve. Add salt to taste.

DANIEL'S BROILER

SHRIMP AND BUTTER LETTUCE SALAD

2 heads butter lettuce
1 cup DRESSING
1 hard-cooked egg,
    shredded

½ pound baby shrimp
1 tomato, sliced in eighths
½ cup croutons

1. Wash lettuce heads well and let dry overnight, inverted on a towel in the refrigerator.
2. When ready to serve, cut or tear the lettuce into 1 to 2-inch pieces into a large mixing bowl. Pour the Dressing over the lettuce and toss lightly until well covered.
3. Portion the salad onto four individual salad plates. Top with the shredded hard-cooked egg, baby shrimp, diced tomato, and croutons.

DRESSING

2 teaspoons tarragon vinegar
Juice of 1 medium-size
    lemon
¼ teaspoon oregano
¼ teaspoon basil

1 egg, coddled 1½ minutes
¼ teaspoon Dijon mustard
¼ teaspoon garlic salt
¾ cup olive oil
Salt and pepper to taste

1. Whip together all ingredients except the olive oil, salt, and pepper in a small mixing bowl.
2. Slowly add the olive oil in a stream, whipping continuously with a wire whisk by hand or on low speed with an electric mixer until the dressing is of a creamy consistency. Finish by adding salt and pepper to taste.

STIR-FRY VEGETABLES AND PRAWNS

24 (16 to 20-count) prawns,
cleaned
1 tablespoon seasoning salt
1 tablespoon finely minced
fresh ginger
1 clove fresh garlic,
minced
1 carrot, cut in julienne
2 stalks celery, sliced
on the diagonal
¼ pound fresh pea pods

½ onion, thinly sliced
¼ pound mushrooms,
thinly sliced
Juice of 2 lemons
¼ cup vermouth
2 tomatoes, halved and
thinly sliced
¼ cup teriyaki sauce
4 teaspoons toasted sesame
seeds
¼ cup chopped green onion
Lemon wedges

1. Add the coconut oil to a sauté pan or wok and place over medium-high heat until the oil is hot. Add the prawns and season with approximately ¾ teaspoon of the seasoning salt. Cook, stirring constantly, until the prawns begin to curl slightly.
2. Stir in the ginger and garlic; sauté for 30 seconds.
3. Stir in the carrot, celery, pea pods, and onion, seasoning lightly again with approximately ½ teaspoon seasoning salt. Sauté for approximately 1 minute.
4. Stir in the sliced mushrooms and the remaining seasoning salt; sauté 1 minute.
5. Add the lemon juice, vermouth, and tomatoes, continuing to sauté for 1 minute longer.
6. Pour in the teriyaki sauce and toss lightly. Turn the mixture out onto a platter, then top with the toasted sesame seeds and green onion. Garnish with lemon wedges around the edge of the platter. Serve immediately.

I like this recipe because it is so quick, so simple to prepare, and yet such an interesting interplay of flavors.

HERBED AND WILD RICE

4 tablespoons clarified
  butter
3 tablespoons finely diced
  onion
2 tablespoons sliced
  mushrooms
  Pinch of thyme
  Pinch of sage
3 ounces wild rice,
  well washed

2 cups Chicken Stock
  (see index)
2 tablespoons vermicelli,
  broken into ¼" pieces
⅓ cup white rice,
  well washed
1 small clove garlic,
  grated
1 teaspoon diced red pepper

1. Heat 3 tablespoons clarified butter in a medium saucepan. Add 1 tablespoon of the onion and the mushrooms and sauté until the onion is soft. Add the thyme and sage; reduce heat and simmer for 5 minutes.
2. Add the wild rice and 1⅓ cups of the chicken stock. Bring to a boil, reduce heat, and simmer 1 hour.
3. Separately, sauté the remaining onion in the remaining clarified butter. When transparent, add the broken vermicelli and white rice. Sauté until lightly browned, stirring constantly and being careful not to burn.
4. Add the grated garlic and sauté for 1 minute more.
5. Add the remaining ⅔ cup chicken stock and bring to a boil. Immediately upon reaching a boil, cover and reduce heat to simmer. Cook 20 minutes without lifting the cover.
6. Stir with a fork, remove from heat, and let stand 5 minutes.
7. Drain off any liquid remaining in the wild rice pan. Allow to cool slightly, then combine with the white rice and diced red pepper. Reheat in a warm oven until ready to serve.

CHOCOLATE MOUSSE PIE

1½ pounds French vanilla
    chocolate (preferably
    Guittard)
1 cup butter
1½ cups whipping cream
10 egg whites

6 egg yolks, lightly beaten
2 tablespoons Grand
    Marnier liqueur
2 tablespoons ground
    walnuts
CRUST

1. Melt the chocolate and butter in the top of a double boiler over medium heat. When melted, stir to blend and set aside to cool. Continue with the preparation only when the chocolate mixture has cooled to slightly above room temperature.
2. Whip the cream until stiff, then set aside. Whip the egg whites until stiff but not dry. Fold the egg whites into the whipped cream.
3. Add the lightly beaten egg yolks to the cooled chocolate mixture; mix well.
4. Gently fold the chocolate mixture into the egg whites and whipped cream. Fold in the Grand Marnier and ground walnuts. Continue folding until the mousse has an even consistency.
5. Spoon the mousse onto the crust and spread evenly in the pan. Shake the pan to remove any air pockets. Chill the pie in the refrigerator for 2 to 4 hours before serving.

DANIEL'S BROILER

CRUST

1 cup graham cracker
  crumbs
3 tablespoons ground
  walnuts

2 tablespoons sugar
¼ teaspoon cinnamon
¼ teaspoon nutmeg
¼ cup butter

Mix all ingredients thoroughly and press firmly into the bottom of a 9-inch springform pan.

Eating this dessert is almost gluttonous because it is so rich. It is a truly hedonistic delight.

Dinner for Six

Foie Gras Salad with Turnips and Spinach

Vineyard Snails with White Wine, Grapes, and Chanterelles

Medallions of Veal with Orange and Lemon

Terrine of White Wine

Wine:

With the Snails—Chateau St. Jean Fumé Blanc, 1980

With the Veal—Château Pontet-Canet, Haut-Médoc, 1976

Four Seasons Hotels, Owner

Roland Baumann, Director of Food and Beverage

THE GEORGIAN

When the Olympic Hotel first opened in 1924, it was hailed as the grandest hotel west of Chicago. Surrounding the old Metropolitan Theater on three sides, the Olympic was built at a cost of 5.5 million dollars by a community of 4,500 Seattle investors on the site of what was once the first building of the University of Washington.

In 1861, Arthur A. Denny, Charles Terry, and Edward Landert, Seattle pioneers, donated ten acres of beautiful land overlooking Elliott Bay to the Territory of Washington to be used for a university site. When the University of Washington moved to northeast Seattle in 1895, it retained ownership of the downtown property which housed its first buildings. To this day, the University owns the land and the Olympic Hotel building, which has been declared an historic monument and is listed on the National Register of Historic Places. In 1980, the Four Seasons Hotels and the Urban Investment and Development Company signed a sixty-year lease with the University, and today, after renovation and restoration, the hotel is known as the Four Seasons Olympic.

The Georgian was the main dining room of the original Olympic, as it is in today's hotel. The room has twenty-four-foot ceilings and magnificent two-story palladian windows which were blacked out during the Second World War and not restored until the 1980s to once again let daylight into the room. It is an elegant room with softly colored fabrics in tones and patterns of peach, putty, and green, with wonderful English Renaissance crystal chandeliers, with beautiful imported marble in abundance, and with baby orchids and delicate Wedgwood bone china on the tables.

The menu of the Georgian is described by Roland Baumann, Director of Food and Beverage, as "international modern cuisine." The philosophy of the Four Seasons Hotel organization is to "use the freshest possible ingredients of whatever area we're in. Our menu here looks very different from the menu of a Four Seasons hotel in Texas or New York." In addition to fresh ingredients of fine quality, Baumann stresses, "we hire the best possible people to prepare the food properly."

The Olympic has a precious history. Six United States Presidents, leaders and princes of many nations have been guests of the hotel. Its ballrooms and restaurants, have witnessed the special occasions of Seattle for over half a century.

411 University Street

FOIE GRAS SALAD WITH TURNIPS AND SPINACH

18 *ounces foie gras*
(goose liver)
6 *ounces turnips*

2 *bunches fresh spinach*
OIL AND VINEGAR
DRESSING

1. Melt a little butter in a sauté pan over moderately high heat. Add the foie gras and sauté until half-done (pink inside), about 4 to 5 minutes. Remove from heat.
2. Cut the turnips in very fine julienne strips. Blanch for 1 minute in boiling water and drain immediately.
3. Wash the spinach thoroughly and dry well. Remove the stems.
4. Combine the julienned turnip and the spinach. Toss with Oil and Vinegar Dressing. Arrange on individual salad plates.
5. Cut the foie gras in julienne sticks, about 1½ inches by ¼ inch by ⅛ inch, or in ¼-inch cubes. Sprinkle over the salads.

OIL AND VINEGAR DRESSING

1 *teaspoon finely chopped*
shallot
½ *teaspoon Dijon mustard*
Salt and pepper to taste

2 *dashes Worcestershire*
sauce
½ *cup red wine vinegar*
¾ *cup olive oil*

1. Combine the shallot, mustard, salt, pepper, Worcestershire sauce, and 2 tablespoons of the vinegar, mixing well.
2. Add the olive oil gradually, blending with a whisk.
3. Add the remaining vinegar, whisking thoroughly.

VINEYARD SNAILS WITH WHITE WINE, GRAPES, AND CHANTERELLES

½ pound chanterelle
  mushrooms
¼ pound butter
36 escargots
1 pound white grapes,
  peeled
½ teaspoon flour

1 cup Riesling wine
2 tablespoons cream
  Salt and pepper to taste
3 drops Worcestershire
  sauce
  Pinch of nutmeg

1. Sauté the chanterelles in 4 tablespoons of the butter for 2 minutes. Remove from the pan with a slotted spoon and set aside.
2. In a separate pan, sauté the snails for 3 to 4 minutes with the remaining 4 tablespoons butter.
3. Add the peeled grapes and sauté for 1 minute more. Add the flour and stir until the butter and flour have blended. Add the chanterelles and the wine and bring to a boil, stirring constantly.
4. When the sauce has thickened slightly, add the cream and return to a boil. Remove from heat.
5. Season with salt, pepper, Worcestershire sauce, and nutmeg.

The key to this recipe is to make the sauce very light and not too thick.

MEDALLIONS OF VEAL WITH ORANGE AND LEMON

3 pounds red potatoes
½ pound butter
  Salt to taste
2 pounds snow peas
12 (4-ounce) slices veal loin
  Flour

Pepper to taste
Juice and zest of 1
  small orange
Juice and zest of 2
  medium lemons

1. Peel the potatoes and cut into ¼-inch cubes.
2. In ¼ pound butter, sauté the potatoes until golden brown on all sides and cooked. Season with salt and set aside.

3. Snap off the ends of the snow peas and remove the strings. Blanch in salted water for 6 to 8 minutes; drain and set aside.

4. Dust the veal slices lightly with flour. Season with salt and pepper to taste. Sauté in ¼ pound butter for approximately 2 minutes on each side, being careful not to overcook.

5. When the veal is cooked, add the juices of the orange and lemons to the pan and bring to a quick boil.

6. Remove the meat from the pan and arrange on dinner plates.

7. Cook the pan juices to reduce by about half. Add the orange and lemon zest.

8. Spoon the sauce over the meat. Arrange the potatoes and the snow peas on the plates and serve.

TERRINE OF WHITE WINE

6 egg yolks
5 tablespoons sugar
1 cup white wine

3½ leaves gelatin (optional)
1 pint whipping cream, whipped

1. Mix the egg yolks and sugar until creamy.

2. Bring the wine to a boil; reduce heat to low and add the sugar/egg mixture. Maintain on low heat, but do not allow to boil, for 3 minutes, stirring constantly. Remove from heat.

3. If using the gelatin, soften in warm water and stir into the egg mixture.

4. Fold in the whipped cream. If gelatin is used, pour into individual molds; otherwise, pour into large wine glasses. Refrigerate at least 1 hour before serving.

Note: The gelatin, if used, produces a more firmly textured terrine. To unmold, set the molds in hot water for 30 seconds, then turn out onto dessert plates.

Leaves of gelatin are far superior to the powdered product.

This is a perfect dessert to be served with sticks of fresh pineapple which have been marinated in plum brandy.

Malia's
NORTHWEST

Dinner for Four

Gravlax with Mustard, Dill, and Honey Sauce

Asparagus and Smoked Salmon with Rémoulade Sauce

Rack of Lamb, Dijon-Style

Salad with Honey, Oil, and Vinegar Dressing

Peanut Butter Pie

Malia's Italian Coffee

Wine:

With the Appetizers—Eyrie Pinot Gris, 1979,
or
Associated Vintners Semillon Blanc, 1980

With the Lamb—Knudsen Erath Pinot Noir, Vintage Select, 1979,
or
A. Rafanelli Zinfandel, 1979

Richard Malia, Owner & Chef

Sharon Kramis, Consultant to Chef

Joe Nix, Chef

MALIA'S NORTHWEST

It would be hard to find a more enthusiastic restaurant owner than Richard Malia. He is constantly visible at Malia's Northwest. He is able to prepare any item on the menu, and sometimes does. He is involved in every detail of what ultimately makes his restaurant an exciting and innovative place to dine.

Richard Malia has a definite philosophy behind his operation. "Only local food can be fresh food," he says, "and we take these fresh products and prepare them interestingly." There is a real emphasis on herbs: "We buy fresh dill, fennel, tarragon, rosemary, and, my favorite, basil." Much thought and creativity are given to which herbs go with which dishes. Malia also buys lamb from packing houses in Ellensburg and obtains an impressive selection of seafood which includes Penn Cove Mussels from Whidbey island, scallops from Oregon, long-line lingcod, Petrale sole and Olympic oysters from Puget Sound, and white king salmon from off the Washington coast.

The peasant cuisines of France and Italy are the inspiration for Malia's menu. "Aristocratic cuisine is very superficial to me," says Malia, "peasant cuisine is the best: it is more interesting, more exciting, heartier, but not as rich, has more depth and more of the soul." But even with all this, his is still basically a Northwest restaurant, offering certain basic favorites and a constantly changing variety of seasonal specialties, such as blueberry cobbler and strawberry and rhubarb tarts.

The decor is as eclectic as the menu is varied. Old Persian carpets grace the hardwood floors of the building that was once the Bank of Germany in the early 1900s and later housed a church. Brown and cream tiles create charming counters and floors in the area. Art-deco lamps, quilted silk wall hangings, tie-back drapes, fresh flowers, potted plants, and musicians playing classical music during dinner hours complete the picture of casual elegance.

Malia's Northwest is a special place to dine. Without modesty, Malia claims to serve "the best food in town for the price." The enthusiasm of its young owner has produced sophisticated, imaginative, yet unpretentious cuisine and ambiance—and, most importantly, a truly Northwest restaurant.

820 Second Avenue

GRAVLAX WITH MUSTARD, DILL, AND HONEY SAUCE

¼ *pound gravlax*
⅓ *cup ballpark mustard*
2 *tablespoons chopped*
    fresh dill

1 *tablespoon honey*

1. Arrange the gravlax attractively on a serving plate.
2. Combine the mustard, dill, and honey, stirring to make a smooth sauce. Serve on the side with the gravlax.

A bed of fresh dill or other greens under the gravlax makes a nice presentation.

We buy our gravlax from Circle C Seafoods in Woodinville. Gravlax is a salmon which is cured in dill and honey under pressure. This is the simplest of appetizers and yet the most delicious.

ASPARAGUS AND SMOKED SALMON
with Rémoulade Sauce

1 *pound large asparagus*
    spears
¼ *pound smoked salmon,*
    in chunks

Green leaf lettuce or
    endive
RÉMOULADE SAUCE
    (see next page)

1. Peel the asparagus skin in strips to give a very tailored look.
2. Blanch the asparagus in a steamer over boiling water for about 1 minute only. Remove and chill.
3. Place the asparagus and smoked salmon on a chilled glass plate garnished with green leaf lettuce or endive. Serve with Rémoulade Sauce.

RÉMOULADE SAUCE

2 egg yolks
1 tablespoon Dijon-style
   mustard
½ teaspoon salt
   Pepper to taste
1¼ cups olive oil
2 tablespoons white vinegar
1 tablespoon tarragon
   vinegar

1 tablespoon dill vinegar
6 tablespoons sour cream
   or yogurt
2 hard-cooked egg yolks, very
   finely chopped (optional)
4 to 6 tablespoons fresh chervil,
   dill, chives, parsley or
   watercress
1 tablespoon chopped parsley

1. Whisk the raw egg yolks, mustard, salt, and pepper in a heavy bowl or blender.
2. Gradually drizzle in the oil, whisking continually, to make an emulsified mayonnaise.
3. Whisk in the vinegars, sour cream, chopped egg yolks, and herb of choice. Garnish the finished sauce with chopped parsley.

RACK OF LAMB, DIJON-STYLE

2 *cups bread crumbs*	¼ *cup olive oil*
¼ *cup butter*	*Cracked peppercorns*
½ *large head fresh garlic*	¼ *cup Dijon mustard*
¼ *cup rosemary*	
4 *(4-rib) racks of lamb, cut*	
French-style	

1. Preheat oven to 425°.
2. Sauté the bread crumbs in the butter, garlic, and rosemary. Don't let the bread crumbs get too greasy or too dry. Set aside.
3. Trim the lamb of all exposed fat and place on a baking dish. Baste with olive oil and sprinkle cracked peppercorns over the top.
4. Place the lamb in preheated oven for about 20 minutes. The inside of the lamb should be rare, about 120°.
5. Pull the lamb out and coat with a thick layer of Dijon mustard and then the seasoned bread crumbs. Cook about another 10 minutes for medium-rare or until done to your desire.

Note: The bread crumbs should be made from 2 to 3-day-old stale bread, rather than bread dried in the oven. They should not be rolled or ground too finely, but should be left as small, coarse chunks.

I would suggest serving the lamb with steamed sugar snap peas, if available, and small, boiled new potatoes, basted with butter and garnished with Parmesan cheese and freshly chopped parsley.

French-style rack of lamb has the fat cut off and the bones are bare.

SALAD WITH HONEY, OIL, AND VINEGAR DRESSING

2 *heads green leaf lettuce*
2 *green onions, very thinly*
   sliced
   HONEY, OIL, AND
   VINEGAR DRESSING

2 *large fresh mushrooms,*
   sliced

Tear the lettuce into bite-sized pieces. Toss lightly with the dressing. Garnish with sliced mushrooms.

HONEY, OIL, AND VINEGAR DRESSING

⅓ *cup rice vinegar*
⅔ *cup olive oil*

1 *tablespoon honey*
1 *teaspoon tamari soy sauce*

Combine all ingredients thoroughly.

This is a very light salad. It is served after the main course to cleanse the palate.

PEANUT BUTTER PIE

½ *pound cream cheese*
1 *cup smooth peanut butter*
1 *cup sugar*
2 *tablespoons butter, melted*
1½ *tablespoons vanilla extract*
1½ *cups heavy cream*

PIE CRUST
3 *ounces milk chocolate,*
   melted
1½ *tablespoons salad oil*
¼ *cup chopped peanuts*

1. Cream the cream cheese, peanut butter, sugar, and melted butter together until smooth.
2. Blend in the vanilla extract and heavy cream.
3. Pour the ingredients into the prepared Pie Crust, smoothing the top. Chill for at least 3 hours.
4. Thin the melted milk chocolate with the salad oil over low heat, then spread quickly over the pie. Garnish with the chopped peanuts. Return to the refrigerator and chill until the chocolate sets.

MALIA'S NORTHWEST

PIE CRUST

1 cup graham cracker crumbs	3½ tablespoons sugar
Pinch of cinnamon	3 tablespoons flour
3 tablespoons cocoa powder	3 tablespoons melted butter

Mix the ingredients together and press firmly into a 9-inch pie pan. Chill until ready to fill.

Some may prefer to substitute semisweet chocolate for the milk chocolate in this pie recipe, but I like the milk chocolate better because it seems to bring out the peanut flavor. Also, I think Mexican vanilla is the best available.

MALIA'S ITALIAN COFFEE

½ pint heavy cream	2 cups gourmet-quality
½ cup Frangelico liqueur	brewed coffee

1. Whip the cream until thickened but not very stiff.
2. Place 2 tablespoons Frangelico in each of four Irish coffee glasses.
3. Add ½ cup brewed coffee to each glass.
4. Float whipped cream to taste on the coffee.

M^cCORMICK'S

FISH HOUSE & BAR

Dinner for Four

Wescott Bay International Petite Oysters on the Half-Shell
Tossed Salad with Creamy Vinaigrette Dressing
King Salmon with Brandy and Peach Sauce
Carrots and Sugar Snap Peas Sauté
Raspberry Sherbet

Wine:
With the Oysters—Korbel Brut champagne
With the Salad—Concannon Sauvignon Blanc
With the Salmon—Chablis Premier Cru, Fourchaume, J. Vercherre
After Dinner—Graham's Vintage Port, 1970

Bill McCormick, Owner
Miles Wilcox, Chef
Gerald Barron, General Manager

MCCORMICK'S

Sitting in McCormick's very quickly transports one back in time and place: the feeling and atmosphere are that of the standard, old-time Boston or New York fish house. Church pews, reminiscent of the late 1800s, with practical and charming coat trees attached, face each other to create most of the seating in the restaurant in private, booth-like units.

Milk-glass school lamps with long brass stems hang from the ceiling, and milk-glass tulip lamps light the tables. Everywhere are framed old photographs, sheet music, and posters. The metal tiles forming the ceiling, the stained glass, and the use of mahogany, oak, and maple in abundance help to complete the feeling of warmth and comfort. "It's an Irish place," states Gerald Barron, the manager, and, indeed, it is.

McCormick's is located in a building constructed in 1912 and originally known as the Oakland Hotel. In January, 1977, Bill McCormick, along with a nucleus of people from his Portland restaurant, Jake's Famous Crawfish, opened the restaurant bearing his name. The philosophy for McCormick's restaurant is stated on the menu: "We take pride in presenting only the highest quality food, prepared totally on the premises." Gerald Barron explains that everything possible is prepared with fresh ingredients. "We have a very small freezer. We don't work out of cans and boxes. We use as many local products as we possibly can, but we also fly in fish from all over the world. Probably a thousand pounds of seafood from the East Coast are flown in each week."

McCormick's has what Barron calls a "living menu." As fresh seafood becomes available seasonally, the menu offerings change. "We try to keep our menu interesting. We also feel the responsibility to educate, to make available new seafoods for people to try." No gimmicks in food or service are allowed. Everything is kept simple on purpose. "We're not trying to dazzle anyone with our saucework or fancy-name dishes," says Barron, and the service, too, is simple and efficient, not meant to impress or overwhelm. "You don't come here for a romantic, candle-light dinner," says Barron. McCormick's is a busy, noisy restaurant and one of the finest places in a seafood town for seafood.

722 Fourth Avenue

WESCOTT BAY INTERNATIONAL PETITE OYSTERS
ON THE HALF-SHELL

16 *fresh Wescott Bay*
   oysters
1 *lemon, cut in wedges*

Parsley sprigs
Tabasco sauce

1. Shuck the oysters just prior to serving, taking care not to damage the delicate meat inside. Be sure to clear the abductor muscle from the bottom of the shell so that the oyster can be easily removed.
2. Serve the oysters on the half-shell set into shaved ice, four to a plate. Garnish with lemon wedges and parsley sprigs and serve Tabasco sauce on the side.

Cocktail sauce may be used, but it would be a shame to mask the flavor of these oysters.

Wescott Bay oysters are grown off San Juan Island. The International Petite is a hybrid cross between the Pacific and the Japanese Kumomoto. These oysters are grown in nets off the floor of the bay and develop a higher meat-to-shell ratio than dredged or raked oysters.

TOSSED SALAD

⅓ *head iceberg lettuce*
⅓ *head romaine lettuce*
⅓ *head Bibb lettuce*
   CREAMY VINAIGRETTE
   DRESSING (see next page)

CROUTONS (see next page)
1 *tomato, sliced*
½ *cucumber, sliced*
½ *cup black olives*

1. Wash and dry the lettuces. Tear the leaves into bite-size pieces.
2. Place the lettuce in a salad bowl and toss gently with the Creamy Vinaigrette Dressing.
3. Portion the salad onto four salad plates. Garnish with Croutons, tomato slices, cucumber slices, and a few black olives.

CREAMY VINAIGRETTE DRESSING

1 tablespoon chopped fresh
   basil
½ tablespoon chopped fresh
   tarragon
  Juice of ½ lemon

2 cloves garlic, pressed
1 tablespoon Dijon mustard
¼ cup red wine vinegar
1 egg
1 cup olive oil

1. In a small bowl, beat the fresh herbs, lemon juice, garlic, and mustard with the vinegar and set aside.
2. In a medium bowl, whip the egg vigorously for 30 seconds; begin gradually adding the oil and then the vinegar mixture until the dressing achieves the consistency of thin mayonnaise.

Fresh herbs will give more flavor if beaten with the vinegar rather than the oil or egg.

CROUTONS

¼ loaf sourdough bread

4 tablespoons butter

Cube the bread and fry until golden in the butter. Drain.

KING SALMON WITH BRANDY AND PEACH SAUCE

¼ pound butter

2 pounds king salmon belly meat, trimmed and cut into 1" slices

4 fresh peaches, sliced in half-moon slices

1 cup julienne-cut leeks, 1½" long

1 tablespoon chopped fresh parsley

Juice of ½ lemon

1½ ounces brandy

¾ cup heavy cream

4 to 6 cups steamed white rice

1. In a large skillet, melt 4 tablespoons butter over medium heat. When the butter has melted and begins to foam, add the salmon. Sauté for about 30 seconds , then add the peaches, leeks, parsley, and lemon juice. Increase the heat and sauté for 45 to 60 seconds.

2. Flame with brandy. After the flame dies, add the cream. Reduce by one-half.

3. Remove from heat and gently stir in the remaining butter to incorporate. Serve at once over steamed white rice.

King salmon is a name given to large chinook salmon. The belly meat is used for this dish due to its high fat content.

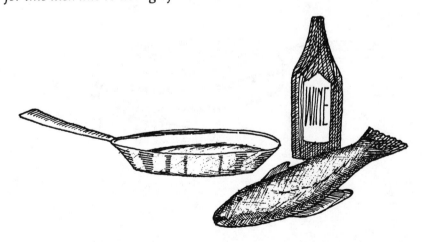

CARROTS AND SUGAR SNAP PEAS SAUTÉ

4 medium-size carrots	White pepper to taste
1 pound sugar snap peas	Salt to taste
¼ cup olive oil	1 clove garlic, very
¼ cup vermouth	finely chopped

1. Cut the carrots into julienne pieces, 1½ inches long and as thin as possible. Steam only until they lose their snap and reach their peak of color, about 1½ to 2 minutes.
2. Wash the peas. Heat the olive oil in a sauté pan until hot. Add the carrots and peas; sauté for 1 to 2 minutes, or just until the peas have reached their peak in color. Deglaze the pan with the vermouth and remove from heat.
3. Season the vegetables with pepper, salt, and garlic.

I like this vegetable combination because it is delicious and adds real color to the plate.

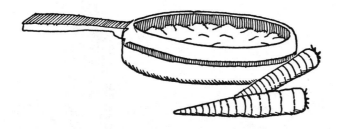

RASPBERRY SHERBET

2 pints fresh raspberries,
   or 1 (10-ounce) package
   frozen
¾ cup sugar

½ cup corn syrup
¼ cup fresh lemon juice
2 egg whites
  Mint leaves

1. Reserve several whole raspberries as garnish. Purée the remainder in a food processor or blender.
2. Dissolve the sugar in 1 cup warm water. Stir in the corn syrup, lemon juice, and raspberry purée.
3. Place this mixture in the freezer and freeze until it sets firm around the edges.
4. In a separate bowl, beat the egg whites until stiff.
5. Turn the partially frozen raspberry mixture in its bowl, then fold in the egg whites.
6. Spoon into individual sorbet glasses and return to the freezer.
7. At serving time, garnish with the reserved raspberries and fresh mint leaves.

Dinner for Four

Smoked Salmon Fettuccini

Chilled Shrimp Gazpacho

Cauliflower and Broccoli Salad

Kal Bi

Sautéed Cucumber with Dill

Brandy Ice ™

Wine:

R. & J. Cook Merlot Blanc

Richard B. Komen, Owner

Tom Speidel, General Manager

Thomas Russell, Assistant Manager

Tim Sullivan, Chef

MORGAN'S LAKEPLACE

In December 1981, Richard B. Komen added Morgan's Lakeplace in Bellevue to his Restaurants Unlimited Organization, which includes Horatio's, Clinkerdagger, Bickerstaff & Pett's, and twelve other eating establishments in Washington, Oregon, California, Alaska, and Hawaii. The goal of the new restaurant, according to Tom Speidel, the general manager, is "to accommodate the lifestyle of the 1980s. Our key slogan is 'foods for all moods.' The menu is structured à la carte so that people can eat as much or as little as they wish." There are over eighty items on the dinner menu, and daily specials emphasizing seasonal, fresh seafood, are available in addition.

Tom Speidel claims, "this is not a stuffy or gimmicky place. We are very straightforward. Fresh, local, quality ingredients are a priority. We try to use the best of everything in our food preparation, yet we try to keep all our menu items, including our wines, very affordable."

Morgan's spaciousness invites the guest to gaze upon the lovely lake through large windows. The openness is accentuated by a black and tan decor against which giant plants in baskets reach to the exposed beams in the cathedral ceilings. Baskets overstuffed with dried weeds add warmth and interest.

Morgan's Lakeplace is actually many restaurants in one. It is a casual place to enjoy lunch or dinner on a sunny day on a deck sitting out over Lake Bellevue, where diners can share their French bread with the always hungry ducks and geese that live there year round. It is a comfortable place to grab a quick snack or light supper before or after a movie or a sporting event: perhaps fettuccini prepared in any one of four ways, or a deep-dish quiche, or a baguette sandwich, or a hamburger. It is a place for celebrating, for lingering over a special meal, accompanied by a well-chosen wine, and ending with a scrumptious dessert. It is a place, as the menu states, that "accommodates unstructured dining." Morgan's is whatever the diner wants it to be.

2 Lake Bellevue Drive

MORGAN'S LAKEPLACE

SMOKED SALMON FETTUCCINI

¼ pound butter
1½ tablespoons minced garlic
1 pint whipping cream
1 teaspoon salt
¼ teaspoon freshly ground pepper
6 tablespoons freshly grated Parmesan cheese

¾ pound fresh fettuccini noodles
1½ ounces smoked salmon, finely chopped
2 teaspoons chopped green onion (¼" pieces)

1. In a heavy-gauge saucepan or a deep frying pan, melt the butter, add the minced garlic, and simmer over low heat for 5 minutes or until the garlic softens.
2. Add the cream, salt, and pepper. Keep the sauce over low heat until it becomes hot and a very low boil forms around the edges of the pan only.
3. When the sauce has reduced by about one-sixth, stir in 3 tablespoons grated Parmesan. Let the sauce stand on low heat.
4. Take the raw fettuccini noodles and separate the strands. Place the pasta in boiling water for approximately 2½ to 3 minutes, stirring twice. The noodles will approximately double in weight. When they have reached desired doneness, strain the noodles into a colander, draining all liquid.
5. Place the noodles in the pan containing the sauce. Stir well to coat, then add the chopped smoked salmon. Stir.
6. Transfer to a heated platter. Top with the remaining 3 tablespoons grated Parmesan and then the chopped green onion. Serve immediately.

When making garlic cream sauce, be sure not to brown the garlic because this will give the sauce a burned flavor. Also, to be sure that the sauce is the correct consistency: when it has reduced down to its thickened form, dip the tip of your finger into the sauce and then hold it upright. The sauce should be thick enough to cling to the fingertip and not run.

MORGAN'S LAKEPLACE

CHILLED SHRIMP GAZPACHO

1 (2") section day-old
  French bread, or 2
  slices white bread
¼ cucumber (approximately)
1 green pepper
3 tablespoons chopped onion
½ tablespoon chopped garlic
7 ounces bloody mary mix
½ pound canned whole
  tomatoes, including juice

1 teaspoon chopped pimiento
2 tablespoons red wine
  vinegar
3 tablespoons olive oil
  Salt and pepper to taste
  Tabasco sauce to taste
2 tablespoons chopped
  green onion (⅛")
6 tablespoons Alaska
  shrimp

1. Cut the bread into 1-inch pieces. Peel and seed the cucumber; dice 2 tablespoons in small (¼-inch) pieces and reserve. Chunk the remainder. Seed the green pepper and chop 2 tablespoons into ¼-inch pieces; reserve. Chunk the remainder.
2. Combine the bread, chunked cucumber and green pepper, the onion, garlic, and bloody mary mix in a food processor. Purée and transfer to a mixing bowl.
3. Drain the canned tomatoes, reserving the juice. Seed the tomatoes and chop into ¼-inch pieces. Add to the purée. Stir in the chopped pimiento, vinegar, olive oil, salt and pepper, Tabasco sauce, and about 7 ounces of the reserved tomato juice. Refrigerate 12 hours.
4. Combine the reserved chopped cucumber and green pepper with the chopped green onion. Refrigerate until ready to serve.
5. To serve, stir the soup well and ladle into chilled bowls. Sprinkle with the chopped vegetables and top with the shrimp. Serve immediately.

CAULIFLOWER AND BROCCOLI SALAD

1 cup cauliflower florets,
     1" by 2"
1 cup broccoli florets,
     1" by 2"

6 tablespoons MUSTARD
     HONEY DRESSING
2 tablespoons sliced roasted
     red peppers

1. Mix together the cauliflower and broccoli florets in a large bowl; add the dressing and toss with spoons to thoroughly coat the vegetables. Let marinate for 2 to 3 hours in the refrigerator.
2. Before serving, re-toss the vegetables. Spoon onto chilled salad plates. Top with the sliced roasted red peppers and serve immediately.

Be sure to shake the dressing very well before pouring over the salad. Any excess dressing may be drained from the vegetables before serving.

MUSTARD HONEY DRESSING

¼ cup white wine vinegar
1 tablespoon prepared
     mustard
½ teaspoon kosher salt
¼ teaspoon freshly ground
     black pepper

¾ teaspoon garlic powder
1 tablespoon honey
⅓ cup salad oil

Combine together all ingredients except the oil in a mixing bowl. While the mixer is turning slowly, gradually add the oil to the other ingredients. Mix for 15 minutes longer. Refrigerate.

KAL BI
Broiled Korean Short Ribs

3½ pounds beef short ribs
cross-cut ½" thick

1½ cups MARINADE

1. Place the ribs in a shallow pan. Pour the marinade over, being sure to completely cover. Cover the pan and let marinate for 2 to 3 days in the refrigerator.
2. When ready to cook, preheat a gas or charcoal broiler to 500°. Drain excess marinade from the meat. Place the ribs on the broiler for approximately 2 minutes, then turn. Cook on the other side for 1 to 2 minutes more, or until the ribs reach desired doneness. Serve on heated plates.

MARINADE

1 cup soy sauce
1 tablespoon minced garlic
1 tablespoon shredded ginger
½ cup sliced green onion
    (⅛" pieces)
1 cup white sugar
½ teaspoon black pepper

2 tablespoons sesame seeds, toasted
½ teaspoon crushed red pepper
2 tablespoons vegetable oil
2 tablespoons sesame oil

Blend together all ingredients except the two oils. Continue to mix the marinade until the sugar is thoroughly dissolved. After the sugar is dissolved, while the mixer is still running, slowly add the oils. Cover and refrigerate for 24 hours to let the flavors blend together well.

Cross-cut short ribs are not always available in the supermarket. You may have to request the meatcutter to do them for you.

Broiling marinated meat can be a sticky business. I suggest that prior to placing the ribs on the broiler, you first wipe the broiler down with a piece of burlap soaked in vegetable oil. This will lubricate the grates and prevent sticking. Also, be sure to turn the ribs promptly or the sugar in the marinade will cause them to char.

SAUTÉED CUCUMBER WITH DILL

4 tablespoons butter	Salt and pepper to taste
2 medium-size cucumbers	
2 teaspoons chopped fresh dill weed	

1. To clarify the butter, melt it over medium heat in a pot. Cool. The solids will sink to the bottom of the pot, and the foam will remain on the top. Skim off the foam. Carefully draw out the clear butter with a ladle, being sure not to disturb the solids on the bottom. Do not stir the butter during this process.
2. Peel the cucumbers. Split in half lengthwise and remove the seeds with a spoon. Slice into ⅜-inch-thick crescents. Refrigerate until ready to serve.
3. Just prior to serving, place a sauté pan over medium-high heat. Ladle in the clarified butter and allow to heat. Add the cucumbers, dill, salt, and pepper. Toss quickly in the pan to coat with hot liquid. When the cucumber is hot, but still crisp, serve.

By clarifying the butter, you will eliminate the solid whey from the sauté pan. The whey will burn at a lower temperature than the rest of the butter, making hot sauté action difficult.

BRANDY ICE ™

3 tablespoons Kahlua	6 tablespoons brandy
3 tablespoons dark crème de cacao	1 quart Dreyer's Grand Vanilla ice cream

1. Mix together the Kahlua, crème de cacao, and brandy.
2. Place small scoops of ice cream in a heavy-duty blender. Use a spoon to break up any large chunks of ice cream.
3. Add the liqueurs to the blender. Using high speed, whip together the ice cream and the liqueurs until smooth and creamy.
4. Chill and serve in pilsner glasses, each with a straw and a long-handled dessert spoon.

Dreyer's Grand ice creams are two percent richer in fat content than their other ice creams, making for a very rich dessert.

Dinner for Four

Moules au Basilic

Crème de Topinambours

Salade Brivoise

Canard Rôti aux Figues

Meringue Framboise

Wine:

With the Mussels—Piesporter Goldtröpfchen

With the Soup—Vouvray, Montcoutour

With the Duck—Chablis Premier Cru, Drouhin

With the Meringue—Château d'Yquem, Sauternes

Park Hilton Hotel, Owner

Paul LeBlanc, Chef

Herman Holland, Maître d'Hôtel

Steve Thorsen, Assistant Maître d'Hôtel

MORILLES

Subtle elegance in a softly formal atmosphere: this is Morilles, in the Park Hilton. A single rosebud in a silver vase adorns each ecru lace tablecloth. Upholstered banquettes in rust line the upper tier of the room, while graceful potted palms, floor-to-ceiling mirrors, and textured wall coverings add softness and warmth to the surroundings. The velvet-jacketed serving staff with their attentive and careful pampering complete the picture of gentle formality.

Chef Paul LeBlanc, who was trained in London, meticulously oversees Morilles's meal preparation and presentation. "We stress quality and care. I purchase the best raw products available to produce the most brilliantly fresh, colorful, and flavorful results for our guests," he asserts. "Every restaurant can say they serve fresh food, but it is what you do with it that makes the difference. We buy the freshest and have the expertise to prepare it properly."

Each evening, Morilles offers a strictly classical French menu, as well as the chef's inspirations of the moment. "The menu is designed à la carte to invite the guest to experience a range of French flavors and textures," explains LeBlanc. The wine list which accompanies the meal presents many Northwest wines, with enough variety to satisfy the most refined palate.

The Sunday brunch at Morilles is a special four-course event, very much like one would find in a fine New Orleans French Quarter restaurant. While a classical guitarist softly strums in the background, freshly squeezed orange juice and grapefruit, warmed and sherried, start the meal. Appetizers, warm or cold, precede the selected entrée. After dessert, miniature bittersweet chocolate cups, filled with amaretto liqueur, vie with previous courses for the pièce de résistance.

"We are an established restaurant, enjoying a strong, repeat clientele," proudly states Herman Holland, maître d'hôtel. "At Morilles, we offer epicurean excellence without intimidation."

The Park Hilton
Sixth and Seneca

MOULES AU BASILIC
Mussels with Basil

FISH FUMET (see next
page) with reserved herbs
½ *cup minced shallots*
1½ *cups white wine*
1 *cup cream*
3 *egg yolks*
Lemon juice to taste

4 *tablespoons butter*
4 *dozen mussels, scrubbed*
and soaked overnight
1 *bunch basil, stemmed*
and coarsely chopped

1. Prepare the Fish Fumet.
2. Place the shallots and 1 cup of the wine in a medium saucepan and simmer until the liquid is reduced by half.
3. Add the fumet and cream and reduce by one-third. Remove the pan from heat.
4. Beat the egg yolks with 2 tablespoons water and stir into the wine/ stock mixture. Stir in the lemon juice. Return to pan to medium heat and whisk constantly until thickened. Do not allow to boil.
5. Separately, melt the butter in a large pan. Add the herbs reserved from the Fish Fumet recipe and the remaining ½ cup white wine. When boiling, add the mussels. Cover and steam until the mussels open. (Discard any mussels that do not open.)
6. Allow the mussels to cool, then inspect and remove any bits of beard that may be left. Return to the liquid in which they were steamed. Simmer until the liquid is reduced to a syrupy consistency.
7. Add the cream sauce and chopped basil and stir to combine. Serve in large soup bowls.

We emphasize the use of fresh herbs at Morilles. With this recipe, the combination of the basil with the shellfish is very complementary.

FISH FUMET

2 *pounds halibut bones*	1 *bay leaf*
1 *carrot, sliced*	1 *sprig fresh thyme*
1 *leek, sliced*	1 *sprig fresh rosemary*
1 *stalk celery, sliced*	4 *tablespoons butter*

1. Place the fish bones, vegetables, herbs, and butter in a stock pot over low heat. Cover and cook, stirring occasionally, until the vegetables are tender.
2. Add water just to cover. Simmer 30 minutes.
3. Strain the broth into another pot, reserving the herbs and discarding the vegetables. Return the broth to medium heat and cook until reduced to 1 cup.

CRÈME DE TOPINAMBOURS
Cream of Jerusalem Artichoke Soup

2 *pounds Jerusalem* *artichokes*	1 *quart Chicken Stock* *(see index)*
½ *baking potato* *Juice of ½ lemon*	¼ to ½ *cup Crème Fraîche* *(see index) or* *heavy cream*
¼ *pound butter*	
½ *yellow onion, thinly sliced*	1 *avocado, thinly sliced*

1. Peel and thinly slice the Jerusalem artichokes and the ½ potato. Place in a bowl of water with the lemon juice as they are sliced. Drain and dry with a towel.
2. Melt the butter in a pot over low heat. Add the artichokes, potato, and onion and simmer for 20 to 30 minutes, stirring occasionally.
3. Add chicken stock just to cover and simmer another 20 minutes.
4. Purée the mixture in a blender or food processor. Add the crème fraîche or cream to thin to desired consistency.
5. Carefully reheat the soup, being sure not to let it boil. Garnish servings with the sliced avocado.

This soup is also good cold. It is a very unique soup; the flavor of the Jerusalem artichokes is enhanced by the purée.

SALADE BRIVOISE
Bibb Lettuce Salad with Walnuts, Oranges, and Raspberries

2 heads Bibb lettuce
2 oranges, peeled
   and sectioned
24 raspberries

12 walnut halves,
   coarsely chopped
DRESSING

1. Wash and thoroughly dry the lettuce. Tear into bite-sized pieces and divide onto four salad plates.
2. Arrange the orange sections and raspberries attractively on top of the lettuce. Sprinkle the chopped walnuts over.
3. Drizzle the desired amount of dressing over the salad and serve.

At Morilles, we serve this salad with julienned duck meat. If you wish, roast a 4 to 5-pound duck according to the directions in the following recipe. Remove the breast and thigh meat and cut in julienne; place over the raspberries as you assemble the salad.

DRESSING

½ cup raspberry vinegar
½ cup walnut oil
¼ cup orange juice
6 sprigs fresh tarragon,
   or ½ teaspoon dried

Salt and freshly
   ground black pepper
   to taste

Thoroughly whisk all ingredients.

Hazelnut oil is a wonderful substitute for walnut oil in this recipe. The oils and the vinegar are available at specialty-foods stores.

CANARD RÔTI AUX FIGUES
Roast Duck with Figs

2 *fresh ducks*
  Salt and pepper to taste
1 *orange, halved*
  Several slices peeled
    fresh gingerroot
  Cayenne pepper to taste
1 *carrot, sliced*
1 *stalk celery, sliced*
½ *onion, sliced*

  Sprig of fresh thyme
  Sprig of fresh rosemary
1 *bay leaf*
½ *cup cognac*
2 *tablespoons julienned*
    fresh gingerroot
4 to 6 *fresh or dried*
    white figs

1. Preheat oven to 375°. Remove the excess fat from each duck. Rinse the cavity and dry well. Season inside the cavity with salt and pepper to taste, then place an orange half and several slices of gingerroot in each. Rub salt and cayenne pepper into the skin. Place the necks and giblets under the ducks to prevent the fat from frying the backs while roasting.
2. Roast for 1 hour, basting frequently and draining off excess fat.
3. Allow the ducks to cool, then split into halves and remove the backbones, rib cages, and wishbones. Prepare a stock with the bones, giblets, root vegetables, and herbs: add water to cover and simmer for 30 to 45 minutes. Strain the stock; return to heat and reduce to 1 cup.
4. Place the duck halves in a roasting pan and prick the skin with a sharp implement. Return to the oven and reheat about 3 to 5 minutes for a pink doneness or cook 30 minutes for a crisp skin.
5. Remove the ducks from the pan. Drain off excess fat and deglaze the pan over medium heat with the cognac and julienned ginger.
6. Slice the figs into round sections. When the stock has been sufficiently reduced, add with the figs to the pan sauce. Stir to blend and remove from heat.

7. Separate the duck legs from the breast pieces. Remove the thigh bones. Arrange the duck pieces on a serving platter, garnished with the glazed fig rounds and julienne of ginger. Dress lightly with the sauce and serve immediately.

This sauce is my inspiration. I have combined two of my favorite flavors, ginger and fig, with the duck. The result is wonderful. At Morilles, we use no roux or cornstarch in our sauces. We use a nouvelle cuisine concept and make all sauces by reduction.

MERINGUE FRAMBOISE
Raspberry Meringue

5 egg whites
¼ cup granulated sugar
⅓ cup ground filberts, toasted
½ cup heavy cream

2 tablespoons Frangelico liqueur
1 cup fresh raspberries
Wildflowers for garnish

1. Preheat oven to 200°.
2. Whip the egg whites to stiff peaks. Fold in the sugar and ground filberts.
3. Pipe or spread the meringue onto a sheet of parchment or rice paper to ⅛-inch thickness. Bake in preheated oven for 30 minutes or until dried out. When done, it should come off the paper easily. Allow to cool, then remove from the paper and break into small pieces.
4. Whip the cream. Fold in the Frangelico and meringue pieces. Place in dessert bowls, top with the raspberries, and garnish with small wildflowers.

My attachment to filberts and raspberries helped me to create this recipe.

Mukilteo Café

Dinner for Four

Smoked Salmon Mousse
or
Pheasant Liver Pâté

Iced Cucumber and Shrimp Soup

Pear-Rosehip Ice

Scallops Bonne Femme

Fennel Root au Gratin

Raspberries Crème Anglaise

Wine:

With the Mousse or Pâté—Lillet apéritif wine

With the Soup—J. Lohr Chenin Blanc

With the Scallops and Fennel—ZD Chardonnay, Santa Barbara, 1979

With the Raspberries—Royal Oporto, 1970

Stein Swenson & Michael Shick, Owners

Steven Parker, Chef

MUKILTEO CAFÉ

One of Stein Swenson's goals was to locate a small site with western exposure and a view. He got precisely that with the Mukilteo Café: sunsets and a pleasing prospect of Puget Sound and the south end of Whidbey Island.

The cafe's menu features a variety of appetizers and entrées. Fresh seafood obtained from local vendors is prepared daily by head chef Steven Parker. Diners may select such delicacies as calamari sauced with garlic and dill, escargot, steamed Race Lagoon mussels, or smoked salmon mousse prepared from the famed Port Chatham lox. The menu also presents Washington-grown lamb and choice beef tenderloin. Fresh and savory vegetable dishes accompany each entrée, and the meal incudes soup, salad, sorbet, and a tantalizing dessert.

Each night before opening, Steven, Stein, and the staff discuss the special dishes to be served and the best choice of wines. During dinner, patrons accordingly receive informed explanations of entrées, complete with wine suggestions. The advice is always friendly and obliging. Stein is present every evening to support this service and to act as host.

He encourages dining in leisure and quiet. And the Mukilteo Café can easily afford that, since it is removed from the hubbub of Seattle activity. For a delightful respite from the city scene and the pressures of a busy day, the restaurant offers the perfect setting.

621 Front Street
Mukilteo

MUKILTEO CAFÉ

SMOKED SALMON MOUSSE

⅛ teaspoon gelatin
2 ounces smoked salmon
  (nova lox)
¾ cup plus 2 tablespoons
  heavy cream
1 teaspoon grated onion

Scant ⅛ teaspoon white pepper
2 drops Tabasco sauce
1 tablespoon chopped fresh
  chives
Salt to taste
SOUR CREAM SAUCE

1. Thoroughly dissolve the gelatin in ¾ tablespoon water in a small bowl or cup.
2. In a food processor fitted with a steel blade or in a blender, purée the smoked salmon with 2 tablespoons cream. Once puréed, press the mixture through a fine sieve into another small bowl.
3. Whip the remaining cream in a separate bowl until stiff. Set aside for a moment.
4. Add the gelatin mixture, onion, pepper, Tabasco sauce, chives, and salt to the salmon purée. Gradually fold in the whipped cream, mixing thoroughly. Taste and adjust seasoning.
5. Spoon the mousse mixture into four (2-ounce) molds or ramekins; tap gently on the table to settle the mixture. Cover and refrigerate overnight.
6. Remove from the molds and serve on beds of Sour Cream Sauce.

SOUR CREAM SAUCE

1 cup sour cream
3 cloves garlic, finely minced
2 tablespoons chopped
  fresh chives

1 tablespoon fresh lemon
  juice
Salt and freshly ground
  white pepper to taste

Combine all ingredients in a small bowl and blend thoroughly.

This sauce is most flavorful if made the day ahead and left to sit overnight. It is equally delicious on fresh steamed vegetables, cold poached fish, and when used as a dressing for cucumber and onion salad.

PHEASANT LIVER PÂTÉ

5 ounces good cognac
1½ ounces ruby port
2 whole bay leaves
1 tablespoon finely chopped
   fresh marjoram, or
   1 teaspoon dried
1 tablespoon finely chopped
   fresh thyme, or
   1 teaspoon dried
1 tablespoon finely chopped
   fresh rosemary, or 1
   teaspoon dried
1 pound pheasant livers
2 tablespoons olive oil
2 tablespoons whole black
   peppercorns

4 cloves garlic, peeled
   and halved
6 shallots, peeled and halved
1 pound pork white fatback,
   plus more to line terrine
¾ pound boneless lean pork
   loin, cut in ½" cubes
¼ pound boneless lean veal,
   cut in ½" cubes
2 carrots, peeled and
   chopped
1 white onion, peeled
   and minced
½ stalk celery, minced
½ teaspoon salt, or to taste

1. Two days before serving, combine 1½ ounces of the cognac, the port, 1 bay leaf, the marjoram, thyme, and rosemary. Add the livers, toss well, and marinate overnight, well covered.
2. Strain the livers and place in a clean bowl. Cover and refrigerate. Preheat oven to 225°.
3. Heat 1 tablespoon of the olive oil in a sauté pan over high heat. When almost smoking, add the peppercorns all at once and stir until they explode. Immediately remove the pan from heat. Add the remaining bay leaf, garlic, and shallots, stirring in the hot pan to burn slightly. Allow to cool.
4. Stir in the livers. Purée in a food processor with a steel blade for 5 to 10 seconds or until smooth. Return to the covered bowl and refrigerate.

5. Cut 1 pound of the fatback in ½-inch cubes. Place the remaining 1 tablespoon olive oil in the sauté pan and heat almost to smoking; add the diced fatback, pork loin, veal, and vegetables. Stir to sear for no more than 2 minutes. Transfer at once to the food processor.

6. Deglaze the pan with the remaining ounce of cognac; add the pan scrapings to the processor. Purée until smooth.

7. Transfer the purée to the bowl of an electric mixer. Whip at high speed until very smooth and almost fluffy. Reduce speed to fairly slow and gradually add the liver purée. When thoroughly blended, sprinkle in the salt and mix well. Cover and place in the refrigerator.

8. Slice the remaining fatback ⅛ inch thick. Line the bottom and sides of a 9-cup terrine mold with the fatback, leaving enough overhang to fold over the top of the pâté. Carefully spoon the pâté mixture into the terrine and fold the fatback over. Place a cover of foil over; top with a block of wood or other weight and, if desired, the terrine lid. Set in a deep pan and add 3 inches of boiling water. Bake in preheated oven for about 5 hours, adding more boiling water every hour.

9. Remove the terrine from the water bath and allow to cool to room temperature. Remove the weights, replace the lid, and refrigerate overnight to set.

10. To serve, remove and discard the fatback lining the terrine. Serve whole or in slices.

Duck or chicken livers, or both, may be substituted for all or part of the pheasant livers. If pork fatback is not available, use thinly sliced fat bacon of the best quality.

ICED CUCUMBER AND SHRIMP SOUP

½ teaspoon gelatin
½ cup Chicken Stock
   (see index)
½ cucumber
¾ cup bay shrimp
½ cup sour cream

1½ teaspoons fresh lemon
   juice
Salt and white pepper
   to taste
¼ cup HOMEMADE
   MAYONNAISE

1. Stir the gelatin into the chicken stock until dissolved. Refrigerate until set.
2. Cut 8 thin slices from the cucumber and reserve for garnish; peel and seed the remainder. Cut into chunks and place in a food processor with the jellied stock. Purée until smooth; remove to a bowl.
3. Reserve 16 shrimp for garnish. Purée the remainder in the processor with ¼ cup sour cream, the lemon juice, salt and pepper, and mayonnaise. Add to the cucumber purée.
4. Add the remaining sour cream to the bowl. Stir thoroughly and taste for seasoning, adjusting if necessary. Refrigerate at least 3 hours before serving. Ladle into small bowls and garnish with the reserved shrimp and cucumber slices.

MUKILTEO CAFÉ

HOMEMADE MAYONNAISE

1 egg, at room temperature
1 tablespoon fresh lemon
   juice
2 teaspoons red wine vinegar
1 teaspoon Dijon-style
   mustard

¼ teaspoon salt
¼ teaspoon white pepper
1 cup olive or vegetable oil
   (or both)

Blend all ingredients except the oil in a blender or food processor at high speed. With the motor running, add the oil very gradually. Whip until thick. Taste for salt, pepper, and lemon and adjust if necessary.

PEAR-ROSEHIP ICE

1½ quarts unsweetened,
   unfiltered pear juice
¼ pound rosehips

Fresh pear slices or
   rose petals

1. Combine the pear juice and the rosehips in a saucepan. Cook on low heat for approximately 15 to 20 minutes, or until the flavors are well combined.
2. Pass the mixture through a fine sieve into a container and freeze.
3. After the mixture has frozen, chip the ice into small pieces and run through a food processor fitted with a steel blade until it is of sorbet consistency. Refreeze.
4. When ready to serve, scrape into chilled wine glasses or sherbet cups. Garnish with fresh pear slices or rose petals.

SCALLOPS BONNE FEMME

½ cup REDUCED FISH FUMET
1½ quarts fresh dairy cream
 (preferably 38% butterfat)
1 tablespoon fresh lemon
 juice
 Freshly ground black
 pepper
2¼ cups dry white wine
6 medium-size shallots,
 finely chopped

1 pound fresh mushrooms,
 thinly sliced
1 tablespoon chopped
 parsley
 Salt
1½ pounds fresh scallops,
 rinsed and dried well
2 tablespoons olive or
 vegetable oil
 Lemon slices or wedges

1. Bring the reduced fumet to a boil in a 2½ or 3-quart saucepan. Add the cream one cup at a time, allowing the mixture to reduce by half after each addition. Add the lemon juice and 1 tablespoon pepper and set aside.

2. In a separate saucepan, bring 2 cups white wine to a boil. Reduce to ¼ cup and add to the cream reduction. The sauce should be thick enough to easily coat a spoon; if not, return to heat and continue to reduce until it will. Strain through a fine sieve. Cover with plastic wrap or waxed paper directly on the surface of the sauce to prevent a "skin"; set aside.

3. Melt 4 tablespoons butter in a skillet over moderately high heat. Add the minced shallots and sauté 1 minute. Add the sliced mushrooms, 2 teaspoons of the chopped parsley, and the remaining ¼ cup wine. Reduce until the liquid has evaporated. Taste and season as desired with salt and pepper. Stir into the cream sauce.

4. If the scallops are large, cut into bite-sized pieces. Rinse and dry the skillet, add the oil and remaining 2 tablespoons butter, and heat over high heat. Add the scallops and sauté only until they turn opaque, about 1 minute. Add to the cream sauce and stir well.

5. Dish onto heated plates or au gratin dishes. Sprinkle with the remaining chopped parsley and garnish with lemon slices or wedges. Serve immediately.

MUKILTEO CAFÉ

REDUCED FISH FUMET

3 leeks, washed and chopped
3 onions, chopped
3 cups dry white wine
   Juice of 1 lemon
1 tablespoon marjoram

1 tablespoon thyme
1 tablespoon rosemary
1 bay leaf
2 pounds halibut bones
   and trimmings

1. Place all ingredients except the fish parts in a large stock pot. Cook over medium heat until the vegetables are soft.
2. Rinse the fish bones and trimmings in a colander and drain; add to the pot. Cook until the bones begin to turn white.
3. Add cold water just to cover. Bring to a boil, skim the surface foam, and reduce heat to simmer. Cook 20 minutes.
4. Pass the liquid through a fine sieve into another saucepan, pressing the fish and vegetables into the sieve to extract as much flavor as possible.
5. Return to a boil. Reduce to ½ cup.

Other white-fleshed fish may be used in place of halibut.

FENNEL ROOT AU GRATIN

1   *(1-pound) fennel root*
2   *cups milk*
¼   *cup butter*
⅓   *cup flour*
3   *tablespoons Pernod liqueur*

2   *cups grated Romano cheese*
1   *cup grated Gruyére cheese*
    Salt and freshly ground
    white pepper to taste

1. Preheat oven to 500°.
2. Slice the fennel root into slices ¼ inch thin. Blanch in boiling salted water until only half cooked—crunchy, but slightly tender.
3. Remove from heat, drain in a colander, dry thoroughly on a towel or paper towels, and place in a buttered au gratin dish. Set aside.
4. In a small saucepan, heat the milk over moderately high heat.
5. In another saucepan, preferably enameled, melt the butter over medium heat. Once melted, add the flour and cook, stirring constantly, for at least 8 minutes, or until the roux smells lightly of oak. Do not allow to brown.
6. Add the hot milk to the roux all at once. Stir vigorously with a whisk. Cook for 2 to 3 minutes over the medium heat; the mixture should thicken nicely.
7. Add the Pernod, 1½ cups Romano cheese, the Gruyére, and salt and pepper. Taste and adjust seasonings if necessary.
8. Pass the sauce through a fine sieve. Cover the fennel root with the sauce. Sprinkle with the remaining ½ cup Romano cheese and bake in preheated oven until bubbly and brown, about 20 minutes.

MUKILTEO CAFÉ

RASPBERRIES CRÈME ANGLAISE

7 egg yolks
1 teaspoon vanilla extract
½ cup sugar

1 quart whole milk
3 cups fresh raspberries

1. In an enameled, heavy-bottomed saucepan large enough to hold all of the ingredients, thoroughly beat together the egg yolks, vanilla extract, and sugar.
2. In a smaller pan, scald the milk over medium heat.
3. Gradually add the hot milk to the egg yolk mixture, whisking constantly to avoid cooking the egg yolks and producing lumps. Cook slowly over medium heat, stirring constantly, until the mixture barely thickens. Pass the mixture through a fine sieve into a bowl. Cover and chill.
5. Place a bed of the crème anglaise on a small plate and place a generous portion of berries atop the crème. Garnish with fresh mint leaves.

This simple, lovely dessert is equally delicious with fresh strawberries, blackberries, peaches, blueberries, or any fruit of choice. When all of the berries are in season, mix and match them, creating an even more stunning color arrangement against the pale crème anglaise.

1904

Dinner for Four

Carpaccio

Spinach and Walnut Salad

Fettuccini Primavera

Salmon with Three-Mustard Sauce

Italian Fruit Tart

Wine:

With the Carpaccio—Charles Shaw Gamay Beaujolais, 1980

With the Salmon—Montagny, Louis Latour, 1979

With the Tart—Domaine Chandon Brut

Andrew Daggatt, David Holt, Illsley Nordstrom, Paul Schell,
& Jim Youngren, Owners

Steve Debaste, Kitchen Manager

Sleek, uncluttered, functional; and not a fern or a potted palm in sight. "The people are the plants," says David Holt, one of 1904, a restaurant with a real urban ambiance. "We intentionally created a stark space; we wanted the people, and not the ferns, to be the atmosphere, to give the restaurant personality."

"Seattle has had restaurants downtown," according to Holt, "but not downtown restaurants." Since the day it opened in 1980, 1904 has been trying to fill a void in the Seattle dining scene. "We are pioneering," explains Holt. "Here is a place where people come and things happen. It is a real gathering place, a place to meet and exchange ideas." Lunchtime in particular finds attorneys, architects, politicians, developers, and others, representing many different lifestyles and careers, conducting business, conversing, and enjoying a creatively prepared meal.

Gordon Walker received a National Architecture Award for his work on the interior of the building at 1904 Fourth Avenue, which was originally constructed in 1906 and is listed in the historical register. The design is unique. A massive wine bar creates the center of the restaurant; it is constructed, as is the staircase leading to the upstairs, of glass bricks with neon behind and industrial pipe. From this wine bar, sixty-five wines by the bottle and thirty-two by the glass are available.

Dinner at 1904 provides a choice of elegant appetizers, including carpaccio, escargot, and pâté, and features fresh pasta—including the house specialty, prepared with smoked salmon, crème fraîche and scotch—in addition to meat, fish, and poultry entrées. "It's actually pretty straightforward stuff," claims Holt. "We try to avoid fancy names and high prices, and we try not to buy anything in a bottle." All of dressings, stocks, desserts, and "the best bread in town" are made in the restaurant.

With the revitalization of the downtown of Seattle, 1904 is in the middle of things, and that seems appropriate for a "downtown" restaurant.

1904 Fourth Avenue

CARPACCIO

1½ *pounds top sirloin roast*
1 *pint SAUCE*

⅔ *cup freshly grated
Parmesan cheese*

1. Cut the top sirloin roast with the grain into logs, 1½ to 2 inches in diameter. Wrap the beef tightly in aluminum foil and freeze. When the meat is frozen, remove and slice into discs as thinly as possible. The more frozen the meat, the easier it is to slice. The meat should be so thin that it is semi-transparent.
2. Arrange the thin discs of meat around the perimeter of a small plate and spread the Sauce in the center of the plate so that it covers the exposed part of the plate.
3. Top sparingly with freshly grated Parmesan cheese and serve.

SAUCE

2 *egg yolks*
1 *cup olive oil*
6 *cloves garlic, minced*
2 *tablespoons Worcestershire
sauce*

¼ *cup red wine vinegar*
1 *teaspoon salt*
¼ *cup Dijon mustard*

1. Proceed as for mayonnaise: whisk the egg yolks until well blended (or blend in a blender), then slowly drizzle in the olive oil.
2. Add the remaining ingredients and blend to amalgamate.

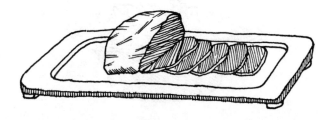

SPINACH AND WALNUT SALAD

2 large bunches fresh spinach
2 cups iceberg lettuce,
   cut in julienne

1¼ cups toasted walnuts,
    skins removed
DRESSING

1. Thoroughly wash and dry the spinach. (If water is left on the spinach, the dressing won't cling to the leaves and also will become diluted.)
2. Tear the spinach into bite-sized pieces and place in a salad bowl.
3. Add the julienned lettuce and 1 cup toasted walnuts.
4. Toss the greens and walnuts with the Dressing. Garnish with the reserved toasted walnuts and serve.

All of our salads, whether they be spinach, Bibb lettuce, or romaine, are hand torn and towel dried. The more moisture left on the greens, the less impact the dressing will have. People generally don't spend enough time on this step.

DRESSING

2 teaspoons Dijon mustard
2 tablespoons white wine
   vinegar
¼ cup walnut oil

2 tablespoons vegetable oil
Coarse black pepper
 to taste
Coarse salt to taste

Blend all ingredients together thoroughly.

FETTUCCINI PRIMAVERA

6 tablespoons olive oil
2 tablespoons butter
½ medium-size onion, thinly sliced
1 sweet red pepper, thinly sliced
1 bunch asparagus, cut in 2" lengths and blanched

½ head broccoli, cut into florets and blanched
1 cup fresh peas
½ pound fresh fettuccini
⅓ cup dry vermouth
Freshly ground black pepper to taste
Freshly grated Parmesan cheese

1. Fill a large pot with water, add ¼ cup olive oil, and bring to a rapid boil.
2. Meanwhile, heat the butter and the remaining 2 tablespoons olive oil in a large sauté pan. Add the onion and sweet red pepper. Lightly sauté.
3. Add the remaining vegetables. Sauté over high heat, tossing continuously.
4. When the vegetables are almost tender, place the pasta in the boiling water. Boil gently for 2 to 3 minutes, or until al dente—soft but with a hint of firmness when bitten.
5. At this point, the vegetables should be crisp-tender. Add the vermouth and continue cooking for 1 to 2 minutes more.
6. Drain the pasta as the vegetables complete their cooking.
7. Toss the vegetables with the fettuccini, adding black pepper to taste. Garnish with grated Parmesan cheese and serve immediately.

The amount of time needed to cook fresh pasta varies greatly, depending on the age, the moisture content, and the quality of the pasta.

SALMON WITH THREE-MUSTARD SAUCE

1 cup Fish Fumet
(see index) or stock
½ cup dry white wine
4 (6 to 8-ounce) fresh
salmon fillets
1½ cups heavy cream
1 heaping tablespoon
Dijon mustard

1 heaping tablespoon
Pommery mustard
1 heaping tablespoon
tarragon mustard
1 teaspoon chopped
fresh tarragon
1 tablespoon butter, cold

1. Preheat the oven to 200°.
2. In a large frying pan, heat the fish fumet and white wine until simmering. Add the salmon fillets, skin side up. Simmer the salmon for 3 to 5 minutes, then turn over.
3. Discard ½ cup of the fumet and add the cream. Bring the mixture to a slow boil. Boil gently for 3 to 4 minutes, or until the fish is firm.
4. Remove the salmon and place in a shallow boat dish; place in the preheated oven until ready to serve.
5. Continue reducing the cream sauce until it thickens enough to cling to the salmon when served. Add the mustards and the tarragon. Blend together over low heat until incorporated.
6. Add the cold butter to finish the sauce. Remove the pan from the heat and swirl the sauce until the butter has melted. Pour over the salmon and serve.

ITALIAN FRUIT TART

1½ cups ricotta cheese
5 tablespoons sugar
1 tablespoon orange liqueur
   Zest of 1 orange
1 tablespoon grated
   semisweet chocolate

SWEET PÂTE BRISÉE
2 pints fresh berries
1 cup red currant jelly

1. Using a food processor, blend together the ricotta cheese, sugar, orange liqueur, orange zest, and grated chocolate.
2. Smooth the filling into the cooled tart shell.
3. Top with the fresh berries.
4. Heat the currant jelly with 1 tablespoon water to make a glaze. Drizzle the glaze over the berries.

SWEET PÂTE BRISÉE

1¼ cups flour
¼ teaspoon salt
2 teaspoons sugar

6 tablespoons cold butter,
   cut into small cubes
1 tablespoon cold margarine

1. Preheat oven to 400°.
2. Combine the flour and the salt in the large bowl of an electric mixer. Add the sugar. With the mixer running, add the cold butter and margarine and then 3 to 4 tablespoons ice water, a tablespoon at a time, until the dough begins to cohere.
3. Chill the dough before rolling to fill an 11-inch tart pan.
4. Bake in preheated oven for 10 to 15 minutes.

You can take advantage of whatever fruit is in season, as we do at 1904. Be adventuresome by using fresh blackberries, strawberries, raspberries, blueberries, or huckleberries; even apples, pears, or peaches would be wonderful in this dessert.

The Palm Court

Dinner for Four

Clams Simmered in White Wine

Cream of Snapper with Mint

Dungeness Crab Legs and Spinach with Raspberry Vinegar Dressing

Veal Medallions with Celery and Madagascar Sauce

Grand Marnier Soufflé

Wine:

With the Crab Legs—Joseph Phelps Fumé Blanc

With the Veal—Clos DuBois Chardonnay,
or
Château Croizet-Bages, Haut-Médoc

Westin Hotel, Owner

Bentley Main, Manager

Reiner Greubel, Executive Chef, Westin Hotel

Marcel Lagnaz, Chef

PALM COURT

T here is probably no restaurant in Seattle more elegant or more sumptuous in decor than the Palm Court, located on the lobby level of the Westin Hotel. Everywhere are mirrors, magnificent crystal chandeliers, and huge potted palms in brass planters. More than half the seating is in the glass atrium, called the Pavilion, which is illuminated at night by a heaven of Tivoli lights. The remaining seating is in comfortably upholstered banquettes lining the upper tier of the room. Persimmon, rust, and taupe color the rich fabric of the brocaded walls, the high-backed upholstered chairs, and the patterned carpeting. Baby orchids in cut crystal vases adorn each table. Only fine china, crystal, and silver are used at each place setting.

A beautiful marble, glass, and brass staircase leads up to Shampers, the English colloquial expression meaning champagne, where one can enjoy a glass of wine chosen from among forty varieties, or a cocktail, with a selection of pâtés or fine cheeses before dining. The intimate lounge overlooks the Palm Court and luxuriously seats fifty in a living-room-like atmosphere.

The Palm Court opened in October 1981, with the goal "to set a new standard for dining in Seattle." A primary objective of the restaurant is to excel in nouvelle cuisine, a trend toward using fresh ingredients and an artistic presentation. Although the emphasis is on basic food, the end result is both exciting and innovative at the Saturday and Sunday brunches and at the nightly dinners.

Under the direction of chef Marcel Lagnaz, who grew up and was educated in Switzerland and has served as chef in fine hotels in Zurich, Manila, Singapore, and London, "each meal is cooked to order with only the freshest and tastiest ingredients, some of which are imported from around the world."

Since the day it opened, the Palm Court has had a goal of excellence. There is a very obvious enthusiasm and pride among the staff as they strive to make the Palm Court "first and best in food and service."

The Westin Hotel
Fifth and Westlake

PALM COURT

CLAMS SIMMERED IN WHITE WINE

½ cup Fish Fumet (see
   index) or stock
½ cup white wine
1 cup brunoise of carrots,
   celery, leek, and onion
2 dozen butter clams,
   thoroughly washed

¾ cup heavy cream
Salt and pepper to taste
Chopped parsley
French bread

1. Combine the fumet or stock, wine, and brunoise in a pan with a tight-fitting cover over high heat. Add the clams, cover, and steam 2 to 4 minutes or until all the clams have opened. (Discard any that will not open.)
2. Remove the clams from the broth and remove the shells. Place the meats in four soup plates.
3. Add the cream to the broth; reduce over medium heat until thickened to a very light sauce consistency. Season to taste with salt and pepper.
4. Pour the sauce over the clams. Sprinkle with parsley and serve with French bread.

Note: A *brunoise* is a very finely diced combination of vegetables, normally including carrot, onion, and celery, used to flavor a broth and give it body.

Mussels are equally wonderful when used in place of clams in this recipe.

CREAM OF SNAPPER WITH MINT

1 cup brunoise of celery,
   carrot, and leek
4 tablespoons butter
¼ cup flour
3 cups Fish Fumet (see
   index) or stock

½ cup white wine
½ pound red snapper, diced
2 teaspoons chopped mint
½ cup heavy cream
¼ cup whipped cream

1. Sauté the brunoise in the butter in a heavy saucepan. When tender, stir in the flour and cook briefly. Do not allow to brown.
2. Add the fumet gradually, stirring constantly. Return to a boil and stir in the wine.
3. Add the snapper and cook just long enough to cook through. Be careful not to overcook or the fish will crumble.
4. Add the mint and heavy cream just before serving.
5. Ladle the soup into individual bowls. Serve with a dollop of whipped cream on each.

Being in the Northwest, which has an abundance of fish, we enjoy preparing and serving this recipe.

DUNGENESS CRAB LEGS AND SPINACH

2 *cups fresh spinach leaves*
32 *mint leaves*
16 *Dungeness crab legs*

RASPBERRY VINEGAR
DRESSING

1. Carefully wash and dry the spinach leaves. Tear into bite-sized pieces.
2. Tear the mint leaves, and then toss the mint with the spinach.
3. Place a handful of the greens on each salad plate. Arrange four crab legs apiece on top of the greens and drizzle with Raspberry Vinegar Dressing to taste.

This is an exotic combination of flavors: the mint with the spinach is very provocative.

RASPBERRY VINEGAR DRESSING

½ *cup raspberry vinegar*
¾ *cup salad oil*
1 *tablespoon chopped*
   shallots

Salt and pepper to taste
Pinch of sugar (optional)

Blend all ingredients thoroughly. If the dressing is too sour, a little sugar may be added.

VEAL MEDALLIONS WITH CELERY AND MADAGASCAR SAUCE

8 (2-ounce) veal medallions
¼ cup flour
6 tablespoons oil
  Salt and pepper to taste
1 celery root
¼ pound butter
1 medium-size carrot, finely diced

½ medium-size onion, finely diced
8 mushrooms, sliced
1 teaspoon pink peppercorns
¾ cup white wine
¾ cup fresh cream or heavy cream
  Lemon juice to taste

1. Dust the veal medallions with flour.
2. Heat the oil in a skillet and brown the medallions on each side. Remove from the pan; season with salt and pepper to taste and keep warm.
3. Cut the celery root in half. Finely dice one half; julienne the other half and reserve.
4. Pour off most of the oil from the skillet. Add 4 tablespoons of the butter to the same skillet. Add the diced vegetables and mushrooms and sauté for 1 minute.
5. Add the peppercorns and the white wine; continue cooking until the sauce is reduced by half.
6. Add the cream, bring to a boil, and continue boiling until the sauce is smooth. Season with salt, pepper, and lemon juice. Stir in the remaining butter.
7. Serve the veal medallions on beds of julienned celery root, coated with sauce.

At the Palm Court we serve two fresh vegetables with lunch and three fresh vegetables with dinner. We no longer serve a starch routinely.

GRAND MARNIER SOUFFLÉ

2 cups milk
½ cup plus 1 tablespoon sugar
½ cup butter
½ cup flour
8 egg yolks
2 teaspoons vanilla extract

6 tablespoons Grand
   Marnier liqueur
4 egg whites
SAUCE

1. Preheat oven to 350°.
2. Bring the milk, sugar, and butter to a boil in a saucepan. As soon as the mixture boils, remove from heat and add the flour all at once. Stir in well. Allow to cool for a few minutes.
3. Add the egg yolks one at a time, stirring well after each addition. Stir in the vanilla extract and Grand Marnier.
4. Beat the egg whites to stiff peaks. Fold in 2 cups of the yolk mixture, discarding any remainder.
5. Divide the batter among four 5-ounce soufflé dishes. Bake in preheated oven for 20 minutes. Prepare the Sauce while the soufflés are baking.
6. Serve immediately upon removing from the oven, with the Sauce on the side.

To make a wonderful Chocolate Soufflé, use the same recipe but omit the Grand Marnier; add 9 ounces melted chocolate and use 5 egg whites instead of 4.

SAUCE

2 egg yolks
½ cup heavy cream

1 teaspoon powdered sugar

Beat the egg yolks, then beat in the cream and powdered sugar.

PETIT CAFÉ

✠✠✠

Dinner for Four

Kir Vermouth

Escargots au Roquefort

Poulet à la Moutarde

Mousse de Poireaux

Navarin de Mouton

Salade Petit Café

Poires Belle-Hélène

Wine:

With the Escargot and Poulet à la Moutarde—Mâcon Lugny, Les Charmes, 1979 or 1980

With the Navarin—Vosne-Romanée, 1977 or 1978

Abel Khemis, Proprietor

Ali Chalal, Chef

Petit Café, an intimate French bistro which seats only twenty-five, is no place to go if you are in a hurry—not due to inattentive service, but because owner Abel Khemis encourages leisurely dining and head chef Ali Chalal cooks each meal to order. Both Abel and Ali came to America after lengthy sojourns in Paris. Abel arrived first and opened Petit Café in December 1977. At that time, he invited his old friend Ali, still a chef in Paris, to be head chef in his Seattle restaurant. Ali came, and in June 1978, the two set about in earnest to accomplish a mutual goal: providing excellent French food and Algerian couscous in a setting of conviviality and relaxation.

Abel was always committed to serving authentic North African cuisine. Couscous grains thus are handled and cooked carefully in the traditional manner. Often serving the guests himself, Abel encourages them to try new items. He explains each dish succinctly, so that guests who are at first reluctant will order exotic dishes like the duck in chocolate sauce or swordfish with sauce à la bordelaise. Ali, an aficionado and quite a master with lamb, will spice a lamb and vegetable mélange with great finesse. He also believes that vegetable side dishes should be an exciting aspect of the meal. He will serve duxelles bound with sauce béchamel stuffed into an artichoke bottom, asparagus spears in puff pastry, or potatoes dauphine.

The regional French dishes range from rabbit variously prepared to stuffed, baked beal to duck in raspberry sauce. Strict attention is given to the unique sauces selected to accompany the fish, poultry, meat, and vegetables. Sauces are thickened through reductions and are subtly seasoned, so that they never overpower the foods they accent.

3410 Northeast 55th Street

PETIT CAFÉ
KIR VERMOUTH

Per serving:

> 1 *ounce crème de cassis*
> 4 to 5 *ounces dry white*
> *vermouth, chilled*

Lemon twist

Measure the crème de cassis into each glass. Fill with the vermouth and add the twist of lemon. Serve with or without ice.

ESCARGOTS AU ROQUEFORT

¼ *pound butter*
3 *ounces Roquefort cheese*
1 *teaspoon dried tarragon,*
  or 1 tablespoon fresh
1 *teaspoon dried chervil,*
  or 1 tablespoon fresh

White pepper
1 *tablespoon brandy*
24 *snails*
¼ *cup bread crumbs*
  French bread

1. Preheat broiler.
2. Place the butter, Roquefort, herbs, pepper, and brandy in a food processor fitted with a steel blade. Process the mixture until thoroughly blended to a paste.
3. Melt the paste in a skillet over low heat—do not boil. Once the paste is melted, add the snails. Stir constantly until heated through.
4. Place six snails on each of four dishes or escargot platters. Divide the sauce evenly over the snails. Sprinkle the bread crumbs over and place under preheated broiler until golden brown, about 2 minutes. Serve with fresh French bread.

POULET A LA MOUTARDE

¼ pound plus 1 tablespoon
　　butter
2 tablespoons vegetable oil
4 (8-ounce) boned and
　　skinned chicken breasts
3 tablespoons cognac
¼ cup minced shallots
1 cup dry white wine

3 tablespoons Dijon-style
　　mustard
Salt and pepper
1 egg yolk
1 teaspoon lemon juice
　　(or more to taste)
1 cup heavy cream

1. In a stainless steel or enameled skillet, melt ¼ pound butter and the oil over moderately high heat. Add the chicken breasts and cook until lightly browned. Remove the chicken to a platter and cover with foil to keep warm.

2. Heat the cognac in the same skillet. Ignite with a match, stirring until the flame dies.

3. Add the remaining 1 tablespoon butter to the pan, allow to melt, and add the minced shallots. Cook, stirring frequently, until lightly browned.

4. Return the chicken to the pan. Combine the wine and mustard and pour the mixture over the chicken. Add salt and pepper to taste. Cover and let simmer until the breasts are resilient when touched and fork tender, about 15 to 20 minutes. Do not overcook to produce a tough, dry fish.

5. Separately, mix the egg yolk, lemon juice, and cream together in a small bowl. Pour the mixture over the breasts in the skillet. Stir this mixture into any liquid that has formed in the skillet and toss the breasts to coat thoroughly. Without boiling, continue to cook for 1 to 2 minutes.

6. Place the breasts on individual heated serving plates and spoon the sauce evenly over each. Serve with Mousse de Poireaux.

MOUSSE DE POIREAUX
Leek Mousse

3 *pounds whole, young leeks*
6 *tablespoons butter*

Salt and freshly ground pepper
1 *cup heavy cream*

1. Remove most of the green stalks from the leeks, leaving only a hint of green near the white portion, if it is tender. Cut lengthwise into fourths and wash very well, removing any grit that may be trapped between the rings. Dry well with paper towels. Chop to a medium dice.
2. Over medium heat, melt 4 tablespoons of the butter in a skillet. When the butter has completely melted and the foam begins to subside, add the chopped leek. Cook about 30 minutes or until soft but not browned, stirring frequently. Add salt and pepper to taste.
3. Transfer the leeks to a food processor fitted with a steel blade. Process for 4 minutes.
4. With the motor running, add the cream through the feed tube and process 1 more minute.
5. Heat the remaining 2 tablespoons butter in a small pan and, after it melts and is slightly brown, pour the butter into the mousse mixture in the processor. Mix well. Taste for salt and pepper, adding more as needed.
6. Keep the mixture warm in a bain-marie until ready to serve.

NAVARIN DE MOUTON

3 carrots	2 bay leaves
4 tablespoons butter	1 stalk celery
2 teaspoons vegetable or olive oil	3 fresh tomatoes, diced
2 onions, coarsely chopped	1 teaspoon thyme
2 pounds boneless leg of lamb, cleaned and cut in 1½" cubes	Salt and pepper
	1 cup dry white wine, plus more as needed
½ cup flour	1 pound turnips, peeled and cubed
1 head garlic	1 pound baby red potatoes, scrubbed
1 leek, white only, halved	
4 sprigs parsley, stems included	

1. Preheat oven to 400°.
2. Slice two of the carrots into circles about ⅛ inch thick. Cut the other carrot in half and reserve for the bouquet garni.
3. Melt the butter with the oil in a large ovenproof skillet over moderately high heat. Add the sliced carrots and chopped onions and sauté for 3 to 4 minutes or until the vegetables have softened but not browned.
4. Add the lamb; brown the meat on all sides. Drain off the excess grease and sprinkle the flour over the pan. Toss to coat the meat and vegetables.
5. Bury the whole garlic head in the mixture. Tie together the reserved carrot, leek, parsley sprigs, bay leaves, and celery with a piece of string and bury the bundle in the mixture. Add the diced tomatoes, thyme, and salt and pepper to taste.
6. Add 2 cups water and the wine. The liquid should just cover the meat; if it does not, add more wine. Place the turnips together on one side of the pan.
7. Cover and bake in preheated oven for 1 hour.
8. Place the baby potatoes together on another side of the pan; re-cover and continue to bake for another 30 minutes or until everything is fork tender.

(continued next page)

9. Remove and discard the garlic and bouquet garni. Remove the turnips and potatoes separately with a slotted spoon. If you wish to strain the pan sauce, remove the meat with a slotted spoon and pour the sauce through a strainer. Serve the lamb, carrots, and onion with plenty of pan sauce and the turnips and potatoes on the side.

Many butchers will be glad to bone a leg of lamb for you. Remove as much fat and connective tissue as possible before cutting the meat into cubes.

SALADE PETIT CAFÉ

3 tablespoons red wine
   vinegar
1 teaspoon chopped garlic
½ to 1 teaspoon tarragon
2 tablespoons Dijon-style
   mustard

1 egg yolk
   Salt and pepper
⅔ cup olive oil or vegetable
   oil (or a combination)
1 head red leaf lettuce, rinsed
   and thoroughly dried

1. Place the first six ingredients in a small bowl. Whisk together.
2. Gradually whisk in the oil. If the mixture is too thick, add a little cold water or more vinegar. If it is too thin, add more oil. Taste and adjust the seasoning.
3. Pour onto the dried greens and toss gently but thoroughly.

POIRES BELLE-HÉLÈNE

2 quarts medium-strength
   Earl Grey tea
2 firm pears (preferably
   d'Anjou)
1 lemon, halved
2 cups chocolate sauce
2 tablespoons triple sec
   liqueur

1 cup heavy cream
1 teaspoon vanilla extract
2 teaspoons confectioners'
   sugar
8 small scoops vanilla
   ice cream

1. Bring the tea to a simmer in an enameled or stainless-steel saucepan over medium heat.
2. Cut each pear in half. Peel, core, and immediately rub the surface with the lemon.
3. Place the pear halves in the hot tea and poach for 3 to 4 minutes on each side, or until tender but still firm. Some varieties of pear will poach faster than others, so keep an eye on them. Remove from the tea with a slotted spoon and set aside to cool.
5. In a separate saucepan, slowly heat the chocolate sauce. Stir in the triple sec; keep warm.
6. Whip the heavy cream to soft peaks. Add the vanilla extract and confectioners' sugar and whip to stiff peaks.
7. Place one pear half on each of four cold serving plates, hollowed side up. Place two scoops of ice cream on each pear half. Drizzle each pear with ½ cup of the heated chocolate sauce (or to taste) and immediately top with a generous dollop of whipped cream.

Settebello

Dinner for Six

Calamaretti Ripieni al Forno

Rigatoni con Prosciutto, Pomodoro, e Cipolla

Scaloppini di Vitello al Vino Marsala e Funghi Freschi

Insalata Fresca di Stagione

Zabaglione al Gusto Frangelico

Beverages:

With the Squid and Pasta—Pinot Grìgio del Trentino

With the Veal and Salad—Barolo or Chianti Clàssico

With the Zabaglione—Vin Santo di Toscana

After Dinner—espresso coffee

SETTEBELLO

Located in a curving, wedge-shaped building overlooking one of Seattle's more interesting city blocks, Settebello displays the modern Italian flair for design. Split levels and low partitions divide the space into a pleasant maze of functional units. Splashes of color and an occasional natural wood finish against the background of greyish shades create a clean, vital atmosphere to complement the cuisine. Along one wall, a narrow kitchen produces the zesty Northern Italian specialties for which the restaurant, in the few months since it opened, has already become famous.

"We strive to use the best produce, the best materials," says owner Luciano Bardinelli. "Each item that we use has its own flavor; we try to bring that out in the preparation. The secret of any good food is to keep it simple—if your materials are good, of course. We produce—at least we think we do—the best Italian cuisine has to offer."

Although Settebello's success has been instant, Bardinelli reminds us that it is the culmination of twenty years of experience with restaurants. Born in Milan, he entered the business at sixteen. After a period in Switzerland, "where I learned to make Steak Tartare the right way," he came to the United States. Before opening Settebello he worked in Los Angeles, Las Vegas, and San Francisco as maître d', manager, and owner. "I've worked mostly out front. Of course, I cook—I can help with the food. I have a lot of love for food and a lot of love for what I do in front.

"The difficulty in opening Settebello was in not knowing how the public here would like what we offer," he says. "I opened a similar restaurant in San Francisco a while back and it was well received, but you can't know what will happen. It's worked very well, though. People here are more appreciative, more sincere in their response to what we do. The people that come here go and tell the chef or the manager that they had a good meal and they enjoyed it. That kind of response escaped me in San Francisco.

"I think I made the right decision, coming to Seattle. I have no regrets for the glamour of Beverly Hills or whatever. I have worked in many, many places where I helped to consolidate their success. Finally I decided to do it my own way."

1525 East Olive Way

CALAMARETTI RIPIENI AL FORNO

12 small squid	Bread crumbs
1 clove garlic	¼ cup olive oil
¼ bunch fresh parsley, chopped (approximately)	Salt and pepper
	½ cup dry white wine

1. Preheat oven to 350°.
2. To clean the squid, remove the cartilage, the black ink sac, and the yellow beak under the head. Rinse in plenty of cold water. Dry with a towel.
3. Detach the tentacles from the "sails." Chop the tentacles with the garlic and parsley, then mix with bread crumbs to taste and enough olive oil to moisten. Season to taste with salt and pepper.
4. Fill the sails with the chopped mixture. Close with toothpicks.
5. Place the remaining olive oil in an ovenproof sauté pan over high heat. When the oil is hot, add the stuffed squid. Moisten with the oil in the pan and season lightly with salt and pepper. Add the wine and place in preheated oven for 12 minutes or until done. Remove the toothpicks and serve immediately.

The secret of any good food is to keep it as simple as you can; and, of course, to use the best materials. You want to give each item a chance to develop its individual flavor.

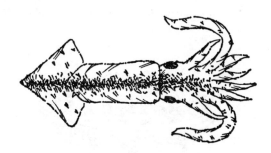

RIGATONI CON PROSCIUTTO, POMODORO, E CIPOLLA

2 *pounds Italian pear
   tomatoes (preferably fresh)*
2 *tablespoons olive oil*
¼ *onion, finely chopped*
   Pinch of crushed red pepper
½ *pound prosciutto ham,
   cut in small julienne*

Salt
2 *pounds rigatoni pasta
   (preferably imported)*
¼ *pound Parmesan cheese,
   freshly grated*

1. If using fresh tomatoes, cut the stem ends out and place in boiling water for about 1 minute to loosen the skins; remove and peel. Cut in julienne and drain well.
2. Bring at least 6 quarts salted water to a rolling boil.
3. Meanwhile, heat the olive oil in a sauté pan over high heat. Add the onion, red pepper, and prosciutto and sauté until the onion becomes lightly golden. Add the tomatoes and salt to taste. Reduce heat and simmer for 8 to 10 mnutes.
4. Add the rigatoni to the rapidly boiling water a little at a time to maintain a rolling boil, but not excessively slowly. Cook al dente, stirring occasionally. Drain and place in a large bowl.
5. Pour the sauce over the pasta. Add the grated cheese, mix well, and serve.

If you are using fresh tomatoes, you will try not to overpower their flavor with a lot of spices—you want the freshness to come through.

SCALOPPINI DI VITELLO AL VINO MARSALA
E FUNGHI FRESCHI

18 *(1½ to 2-ounce) scaloppini*
   of veal loin
Salt and pepper
Flour for dredging

¾ *pound butter*
2 *cups Marsala wine*
1 *pound fresh mushrooms,*
   sliced

1. Season the veal with salt and pepper and then dredge very lightly in flour.
2. Melt ½ pound butter in a very large sauté pan over low heat. Add the veal; raise the heat to high and sauté on both sides until golden.
3. Add the Marsala and allow to reduce by four-fifths, still over high heat. Remove the veal to a heated serving plate.
4. Add 1 tablespoon water and the remaining ¼ pound butter to the pan. When hot, add the sliced mushrooms and sauté rapidly for 1 to 2 minutes. Cover the scaloppini with the sauce and serve immediately.

Note: if you don't have a pan large enough to hold all the scaloppini in one layer, you may cook the veal in stages, adding butter as needed.

INSALATINA FRESCA DI STAGIONE

3 heads soft-textured
   lettuce in season
2 pinches salt
1 pinch black pepper

1 tablespoon red wine
   vinegar
3 tablespoons olive oil

Wash the lettuce and dry well. Tear into large pieces and place in a salad bowl. Add the salt and pepper, then the vinegar and oil. Toss lightly and serve.

Bibb lettuce or endive are examples of greens for this salad.

SETTEBELLO

ZABAGLIONE AL GUSTO FRANGELICO

12 eggs, separated
6 tablespoons sugar

¼ cup Frangelico liqueur

1. In the top of a large double boiler, beat the egg whites until stiff.
2. Add the egg yolks and place over boiling water, beating constantly until firm enough that the whisk leaves a ribbon lasting a few seconds on the surface of the mixture.
3. Add the Frangelico and continue to beat until the mixture has the consistency of a soft custard. Take care not to overcook; the eggs will scramble if cooked too long. Serve immediately.

The Vine Street

Dinner for Six

Moules à la Marinière

Potage Crème de Champignons

Saumon Princesse

Choux Brocolis Blanchis au Beurre au Citron

Gâteau de Fromage au Chocolat

Wine:

a white Bordeaux

James & Shirley Houston, Owners

Lee Ratcliffe, Executive chef

Daniel Wakgira, Manager

VINE STREET RESTAURANT

On Christmas Day, 1979, James and Shirley Houston became the owners of a restaurant located in a modest stucco building that is a historical landmark. The Vine Street Restaurant and Lounge emerged as a charming, intimate, and unpretentious place to linger over dinner or lunch in what was once the main floor of a building which was erected for the Alaska-Yukon Exposition of 1909 and which later became the Belltown Hospital. The Houstons' philosophy has been simple and straightforward since that first Christmas Day of ownership: "The food is the most important thing. We strive to be consistent. People who dine here know that the excellent meal enjoyed at one visit will be just as fine the next time it is ordered."

The restaurant is not large. Only about forty-five can be seated in the dining room which is warmly nestled against a wall of old brick that dates back to the building's beginning. The walls are covered with paintings, some mammoth, some small, all colorfully imitating Toulouse-Lautrec. Gracing the walls of the bar and private banquet room are the especially beautiful, large and stately gold-leaf-framed Louis XVI mirrors which the owners obtained from the Carnegie estate. In the dining room, the yellow and white daisy centerpieces on the tablecloths contrast nicely with the old, unmatched ladder-back chairs that frame the sometimes round, sometimes square tables. Four large, cozy booths are also available, and on sunny days in the spring and summer both lunch and dinner are served outdoors.

The menu is basically French with the emphasis on nouvelle cuisine, but occasionally a German or Italian pièce de résistance will be available to the diners' delight. Each meal is prepared under the supervision of Lee Ratcliffe, the chef-manager, who says, "I aim for the freshest of ingredients, with the exception of a few imported products. My goal is to create a dish that will first be appealing to the eye, but ultimately to the palate. My greatest satisfaction is hearing someone say how much he has enjoyed his meal."

2600 First Avenue

VINE STREET RESTAURANT

MOULES A LA MARINIÈRE

6 quarts Penn Cove mussels
2 cups minced shallots
   or chopped onions
3 cups dry white wine
   or dry vermouth
1 tablespoon white vinegar
1 teaspoon thyme
4 bay leaves
¼ teaspoon salt

¼ teaspoon freshly ground
   black pepper
1 clove garlic, minced
5 sprigs parsley
⅓ cup cream or butter
½ cup chopped parsley
   Lemon wedges
   French or sourdough bread

1. Use fresh mussels only—ones with their shells tightly closed. Discard any shell which is open. Scrub the mussels with a vegetable brush under running water. Hold the mussel firmly in one hand with the pointed end up, grasp the *byssus*—or "beard"—firmly, and pull down and out. The beard should pull out cleanly. If a stub of the beard stays behind, cut it close to the shell with a knife or remove it after cooking. Set the mussels in a basin or bucket of fresh water for 1 to 2 hours so they will disgorge their sand and also lose a bit of their saltiness. Place in a colander, wash, and drain again.
2. Combine all the ingredients except the mussels, cream or butter, parsley, lemon wedges, and bread in a large kettle. Bring to a boil, reduce heat, and simmer for 3 to 5 minutes.
3. Add the mussels, cover, and return to a boil. Steam about 5 minutes, tossing once or twice with a spoon. This will open the mussels and mix the ingredients. After 5 minutes, all the mussels should be gaping wide. Discard any mussels with shells which have not opened.
4. With a large spoon, scoop the mussels into individual serving bowls. Strain the broth into a mixing bowl. Add the cream or butter, chopped parsley, and salt and pepper to taste. Pour the sauce over the mussels in the bowls.
5. Serve with lemon wedges and generous portions of French or sourdough bread for dunking in the broth.

There is just enough of the mussel flavor in the broth so that when you dip the bread it is a delight.

POTAGE CRÈME DE CHAMPIGNONS

1½ pounds firm, white mushrooms, cleaned
2 small lemons, or 1 large
1 tablespoon unsalted butter
3 tablespoons minced shallots
⅓ teaspoon dried thyme
1 bay leaf
1 teaspoon salt
¾ teaspoon freshly ground pepper
3 cups heavy cream
2½ cups CHICKEN STOCK
¼ cup sherry
1½ teaspoons cornstarch
2 tablespoons minced parsley

1. Sprinkle the mushrooms with the lemon juice. Chop coarsely.
2. Melt the butter in a saucepan and lightly sauté the shallots. Add the mushrooms, thyme, and bay leaf; sauté over moderate heat for 10 minutes, or until the liquid disappears.
3. Add the salt, pepper, cream, chicken stock, and sherry and bring to a boil. Reduce heat and simmer for 20 minutes.
4. Dissolve the cornstarch in 1 tablespoon water and stir into the soup. Continue to simmer for 10 minutes longer, stirring constantly. Correct seasoning to taste. Serve in warmed bowls. Sprinkle with minced parsley.

This soup is very simple and easy to make, but be careful not to overcook it.

VINE STREET RESTAURANT

CHICKEN STOCK

Makes about 6 cups.

1 (4-pound) chicken,
   quartered, with giblets
1 pound veal bones, cracked
1 large onion, stuck
   with 2 cloves
2 leeks, split and washed
   well
2 carrots, cut in half

1 stalk celery, cut in half
2 teaspoons salt
   Bouquet garni:
   6 sprigs parsley
   2 sprigs thyme, or
    1 teaspoon dried
   1 clove garlic, peeled
   1 bay leaf

1. Remove the skin and fat from the chicken. Place the chicken in a stock pot with the giblets, but not the liver. Add the veal bones and 3 quarts water and bring to a boil.
2. Reduce heat to low and skim the froth that rises to the surface.
3. Add the onion, leeks, carrots, celery, salt, and bouquet garni. Simmer, skimming the froth as it rises, for 2 hours.
4. Remove the chicken from the pot. Remove the meat from the carcass and reserve for another use. Return the carcass to the broth and simmer another 2 hours, adding boiling water as needed to keep the ingredients covered.
5. Strain the stock, pressing the solids against the sieve to extract their juices. Allow to cool. Refrigerate until the fat congeals; remove the fat and discard. Freeze and use as needed.

The lamb bones are an excellent source of gelatin.

SAUMON PRINCESSE

30 asparagus spears
3 cups white wine
2 to 3 tablespoons minced
   shallots
Juice of 1 lemon
Pinch of salt
Pinch of freshly ground
   black pepper

6 (5-ounce) fillets
   king salmon
3 cups heavy cream
1 teaspoon unsalted butter
   Chopped truffle (optional)

1. Trim the asparagus to 3-inch lengths. Steam until crisp-tender; set aside.
2. Combine the wine, shallots, lemon juice, salt, and pepper in a large pan. Bring to a boil and reduce heat to simmer.
3. Poach the salmon fillets in the wine bouillon for 5 minutes or until done. Remove the salmon and keep warm in a covered dish.
4. Return the bouillon to heat. Add the cream and reduce until thick enough to coat a cooking spoon. Season with salt, pepper, and lemon juice to taste.
5. Add the unsalted butter and mix until smooth. Place the cooked asparagus in the sauce to warm.
6. Place a salmon fillet on each plate. Garnish each with five warmed asparagus spears and the chopped truffle, if desired. Spoon the sauce over and serve.

This recipe is wonderful for the delicate balance of flavorings between the sauce, the asparagus, the salmon, and, if it is used, the truffle.

CHOUX BROCOLIS BLANCHIS AU BEURRE AU CITRON

2 *bunches fresh broccoli,*
   cut, stems peeled,
   and washed

3 *tablespoons salt*
   LEMON BUTTER SAUCE

1. Place the broccoli in a wire salad basket and plunge into at least 6 quarts rapidly boiling salted water over highest heat. As soon as the water returns to a boil again, reduce heat to a light boil and cook for 4 to 6 minutes or until crisp-tender.
2. Remove immediately and place on a serving platter. Pour the Lemon Butter Sauce over.

LEMON BUTTER SAUCE

¼ *cup lemon juice*
⅛ *teaspoon salt*
   Pinch of white pepper
¼ *pound butter, chilled*

2 to 3 *tablespoons fish or*
        vegetable stock, hot,
        or hot water

1. Boil down the lemon juice with the salt and white pepper until reduced to 1 tablespoon. Remove from heat and immediately beat in 2 tablespoons of the chilled butter.
2. Set over very low heat and beat in the remaining 6 tablespoons chilled butter, a piece at a time, to make a creamy, thick sauce. Immediately remove from heat.
3. Just before serving, beat in 2 to 3 tablespoons hot fish or vegetable stock or hot water, a few drops at a time, to warm the sauce. Correct seasoning to taste.

GÂTEAU DE FROMAGE AU CHOCOLAT

10 ounces cream cheese,
  at room temperature
⅔ cup cocoa powder
2 cups granulated sugar
2 teaspoons vanilla extract
6 tablespoons orange-
  flavored liqueur
4 eggs
  GRAHAM CRACKER
  CRUST

1¾ cups sour cream
⅓ cup hazelnuts, very
  finely chopped
⅓ cup almonds, very
  finely chopped
  Whole hazelnuts or
  sliced almonds

1. Preheat oven to 375°.
2. With a wooden spoon, cream the cream cheese and ⅓ cup of the cocoa together until smooth.
3. Add 1 cup sugar, 1 teaspoon vanilla extract, and 3 tablespoons liqueur and blend until smooth. Add the eggs one at a time, blending until smooth after each addition.
4. Spread evenly in the prepared crust and place in a bain-marie. Bake in preheated oven for 30 to 40 minutes, or until the center is firm to the touch. Remove from oven and cool 10 to 15 minutes.
5. Combine the sour cream with the remaining cocoa, sugar, vanilla extract, and liqueur, blending until smooth.
6. Add the chopped hazelnuts and almonds and blend. Spread the mixture over the cooled bottom layer.
7. Replace in the bain-marie and bake for another 20 to 25 minutes, or until firm. About 5 minutes before the gâteau is done, decorate the top with whole hazelnuts or sliced almonds.
8. Allow to set at room temperature for 10 to 20 minutes. Place in refrigerator until chilled before serving.

It is important not to overbake this dessert or the sour cream will curdle and the cake will become crumbly.

VINE STREET RESTAURANT

GRAHAM CRACKER CRUST

1 cup graham cracker
  crumbs
6 tablespoons unsalted
  butter

½ teaspoon nutmeg
½ teaspoon cinnamon

Preheat oven to 350°. Thoroughly combine the graham cracker crumbs, butter, nutmeg, and cinnamon and press firmly into the bottom and sides of an 8 or 9-inch springform pan. Bake in preheated oven for 2 to 3 minutes. Remove and allow to cool.

Washington POST Cafe

Dinner for Four

Calamari Sauté

Fresh Greens Salad

Post Cafe Bread

Chicken Pommery

Broccoli, Carrots, and Dill Sauté

Steamed New Potatoes with Parsley

Stuffed Baked Apples

Wine:

With the Calamari—Château Martouret, white Bordeaux, 1980

With the Chicken—Château Rolland, Bordeaux, 1980

Mary Kaye Scheldt, Owner

Hugh Kohl & Anne Schwendiman, Chefs

Nance Matthews, Manager

WASHINGTON POST CAFE

The basement of the Post Building, in the space that is rumored to have once been a blacksmith's shop in the early days of Seattle, is now home of the Washington Post Cafe. The charming cafe moved to this historic building two years ago from its original location in the Fremont district.

The first Post Building was destroyed by the Seattle fire of 1889; the present building was constructed soon after that catastrophe and served as the Post Hotel for many years. Today, the restaurant's interior nestles up against a wall of used brick in which the arched window alcoves have been updated and made functional with upholstered cushions for cloistered seating. An ensemble of pipes and valves, which were part of the aged building's cooling and heating system, reign over one section of the restaurant, reminding the visitors that this is, indeed, a part of old Seattle.

This is not a large restaurant. "We are small enough to treat people individually," says Mary Kaye Scheldt, the owner. "We really aim to make everyone feel comfortable and at ease. We want each person to feel better for being here."

Mary Kaye relates to the philosophy of country French cooking. "You prepare what is growing, in the time of year in which it is growing. Our location is close to the market and to the water; both influence what we serve." Emphasizing fresh seasonal seafood, fresh pasta, prepared in several different and interesting ways, the use of herbs and garlic, but very little salt, and always changing chef's specials, the menu takes advantage of the best that the Pike Place Market has to offer daily.

Whether it is for breakfast, weekend brunch, lunch, or dinner, Mary Kay asserts, "we are small and care so much about what comes out of our kitchen. I think our food is exceptional because it is fresh and because it is not what one would cook in one's own home everyday. We are hard to get to, by virtue of being downstairs, but I think we are worth the trip."

88 Yesler Way

CALIMARI SAUTÉ

12 squid, cleaned and cut crosswise in ¼" rings	1 tablespoon finely chopped parsley
4 to 6 tablespoons olive oil	2 tablespoons butter
¾ tablespoon oregano	¼ cup white wine
1½ teaspoons thyme	Juice of 1 lemon
1 tomato, chopped	Lemon wedges
4 to 6 cloves garlic, minced	Bread and unsalted butter

1. Sauté the squid quickly over high heat in the olive oil with oregano and thyme.
2. Reduce heat slightly and add the remaining ingredients except the lemon, bread, and butter. Simmer briefly to heat completely.
3. Garnish with lemon wedges. Serve at once with fresh bread and unsalted butter.

Your fishmonger can be your best friend if you have not cleaned calamari before.

FRESH GREENS SALAD

1 large head romaine, cleaned and torn into bite-size pieces	1 red, ripe tomato, cored and cut into eighths
Greens of choice	Freshly grated Parmesan cheese
TARRAGON VINAIGRETTE DRESSING (see next page)	Bleu cheese, crumbled (optional)

1. Gently toss the romaine and your greens of choice with the Tarragon Vinaigrette Dressing.
2. Add the tomato and toss only to coat with dressing.
3. Garnish with the Parmesan cheese and bleu cheese if desired. Serve immediately.

Use any of the season's vegetables as part of the greens: garden-fresh zucchini, cut julienne; Italian parsley; fresh mint or other herbs.

TARRAGON VINAIGRETTE DRESSING

¾ cup soy oil, or
   any other light oil
4 to 6 tablespoons white wine
   vinegar
1½ teaspoons Dijon mustard
1½ teaspoons dried tarragon,
   or 1 tablespoon fresh

1 scallion
Salt (optional)
Freshly ground pepper
   to taste
2 tablespoons Crème Fraîche
   (see index) or sour cream

1. Place all ingredients except the crème fraîche or sour cream in a blender or food processor. Blend in on and off pulses until the scallion is completely minced.
2. Whisk in the crème fraîche or sour cream.

POST CAFE BREAD

Makes 3 loaves.

3 cups milk
6 to 8 tablespoons butter
   or light oil
3 tablespoons yeast
¼ cup sugar

8 cups unbleached white
   flour
3 cups whole wheat flour
2 tablespoons sea salt
1 egg

1. Scald the milk. Add the butter and remove from heat; set aside.
2. Place 1 cup plus 2 tablespoons warm water (about 100°) in a small bowl. Sprinkle the yeast over, then add the sugar. Set aside for 5 to 10 minutes.
3. Combine both flours and the salt. Add the scalded milk and the yeast mixture and stir until the dough comes away from the bowl.
4. Turn out onto a lightly floured board and knead until smooth. Set in a lightly oiled bowl, cover with a towel, and leave in a warm place (72° to 75°) to rise until doubled in bulk.
5. Punch the dough down with your fist and allow to rise another 15 minutes. Preheat oven to 350°.

6. Divide into three sections and shape into loaves. Place in oiled loaf pans and allow to rise another 25 minutes.
7. Beat the egg with 1 tablespoon water. Brush the tops of the loaves with the mixture and bake in preheated oven 20 to 30 minutes or until golden and done.

This bread is well worth the effort of making. We find it a delicious change from French or sourdough breads.

CHICKEN POMMERY

2 tablespoons oil	6 tablespoons Pommery mustard
2 tablespoons butter	½ cup Madeira
2 chicken breasts, split, skinned, and boned	½ cup Chicken Stock (see index)
½ red onion, chopped	1½ cups heavy cream
2 cups mushrooms, sliced	
4 cloves garlic, finely minced	

1. Heat a sauté pan; add the oil, then the butter. When the foam subsides, add the chicken and sauté over moderately high heat until golden brown on one side. Do not turn the chicken.
2. Add the onion, mushrooms, garlic, and mustard. Turn the chicken and finish cooking. Remove to a warmed platter.
3. Working quickly, deglaze the pan over high heat with Madeira and chicken stock.
4. Over moderately high heat, add the heavy cream and reduce until thickened.
5. Pour the sauce over the chicken. Serve with Broccoli, Carrots, and Dill Sauté.

My secret for producing chicken that is tender and uniformly cooked is to lightly pound the breast before cooking. It is also important not to overcook the chicken.

BROCCOLI, CARROTS, AND DILL SAUTÉ

2 *pounds broccoli, cleaned*	*Salt to taste*
6 *carrots, peeled*	4 *tablespoons butter*
and trimmed	¾ *teaspoon dill weed*

1. Cut off and discard the ends of broccoli stalks. Peel the tough outer skins from the stalks close to flower. Slice lengthwise into ⅜ to ½-inch-thick "trees."
2. Slice the carrots lengthwise into ⅜-inch-thick pieces.
3. Bring enough water to cover the vegetables to a boil. Add salt to taste. Parboil the broccoli and carrots until the broccoli turns bright green—just a few minutes. Drain immediately in a colander and refresh briefly under cold water. Drain again thoroughly.
4. While the vegetables are cooking, heat the butter. As it begins to foam, add the dill. Next, add the broccoli and carrots, turning gently to coat. Cover and finish cooking for 2 to 3 minutes, or until barely fork tender.

STEAMED NEW POTATOES WITH PARSLEY

1½ *pounds small new potatoes*	*Salt and freshly ground*
6 *tablespoons butter*	*pepper to taste*
¼ *cup finely chopped parsley*	

1. Steam the potatoes over low heat just until tender: their size will determine the time.
2. When done, drain well and place back on a warm burner. Immediately add the butter and cover the pan with a linen dish towel, placing the lid over the towel. Leave for 5 to 10 minutes. This process absorbs excess moisture and prevents soggy potatoes.
3. When ready to serve, add the parsley and season to taste with salt and freshly ground pepper. Toss well and serve.

STUFFED BAKED APPLES

4 Golden Delicious apples
½ cup coarsely chopped walnuts
¼ cup brown sugar
1 teaspoon grated orange peel
1 teaspoon cinnamon
½ teaspoon finely minced fresh ginger
¼ teaspoon ground cardamom

½ cup raisins
6 tablespoons unsalted butter
2 tablespoons honey
2 tablespoons Grand Marnier liqueur
Juice of 2 oranges
Crème Fraîche (see index) or ice cream

1. Preheat oven to 350°.
2. Core the apples, leaving a ¾-inch plug at the bottom. (A melon scoop is a good tool to use.)
3. Place the nuts, sugar, orange peel, spices, raisins, and butter in a food processor. Process with on and off pulses until a thick paste is formed. Fill the apples with this mixture.
4. Combine the honey, Grand Marnier, and orange juice.
5. Place the apples in a buttered baking dish. Bake in preheated oven for 45 minutes, basting frequently with the honey mixture.
6. Serve with crème fraîche or ice cream.

This is a light dessert which is delicious after any dinner.

"THE WOK"

Dinner for Four

Fried Shrimp Balls

Hot and Pungent Soup

Moo Shu Pork

Hunan Beef

Hot and Spicy Shrimp

Shi Hu Duck

Fried Rose Bananas

Beverages:

Pinot Chardonnay
or
Wan Fu
or
Tsingtao

Mr. and Mrs. Chen, Mr. and Mrs. Andy Ma,

Jemmy Ma & John Yea, Proprietors

THE WOK

T his family-owned and -operated Hunan-Szechuan restaurant, nestled among the clinics surrounding Swedish Hospital, achieved popularity and acclaim almost immediately upon opening its doors in December, 1979. Its cuisine, derived from two of China's colder, mountainous provinces, is noted for its highly peppered dishes. What may escape notice when one's attention is thus diverted is the manner in which the foods' own flavors are brought out and complemented by the various combinations of seasonings, only one element of which are the famous hot peppers. The result is a playground for the palate, an assembly of robust flavors that overpower neither each other nor the natural taste of the fresh ingredients, and the staff of the Wok is happy to adjust the use of hot peppers to enable any palate to enjoy it. Nonetheless, the quintessence of this cuisine is its hotness, and it is recommended that one stretch the boundaries of one's timidity to savor it.

Co-owner and chef Andy Ma supervises the kitchen very closely, and indeed does most of the preparation himself. A battery of woks fitted over specially designed gas flame pits produces a consistent temperature of sixteen hundred degrees; the food, therefore, is cooked very rapidly, preserving the flavor and texture of the carefully selected ingredients. At these extremely high temperatures, the flavors of the seasonings, too, are liberated and combined without losing their identities. The characteristic Hunan-Szechuan hotness is achieved through the use of special peppers that the Wok imports directly from Taiwan.

Jemmy Ma, Andy's Brother, manages the dining room. The service, under his attentive eye, is efficient yet gracious. Often, customers' confidence is engaged enough to allow Jemmy to order for them—which usually means exposure to excellent items that are not on the menu.

The Ma family, originally from Hunan and Szechuan, came to Seattle by way of Taiwan and New York. Both the Mas and the Chens were restaurateurs in New York for several years. In the late seventies, they agreed on a move. Mr. Chen was dispatched to scout the Seattle area— he must have liked it, and Seattle is pleased to return the compliment.

1301 Columbia Street

FRIED SHRIMP BALLS

¾ pound baby shrimp
2 tablespoons lard, chilled
  and finely chopped
½ teaspoon salt
½ teaspoon MSG
½ teaspoon black pepper
½ teaspoon sesame oil

1½ teaspoons rice vinegar
1 tablespoon cornstarch
1 tablespoon flour
1 egg white
6 cups vegetable oil
  Chinese chili paste

1. Rinse and drain the shrimp and dry with a clean tea towel or paper towels. Place in a medium mixing bowl.
2. Add the lard and salt. With a knife or sharp pastry cutter or in a blender or food processor, mash the three ingredients until a smooth paste is produced.
3. Add the remaining ingredients except the oil and chili paste. Blend thoroughly.
4. Heat the oil to 375° in a wok.
5. With your hands, make 1-inch balls out of the shrimp mixture. Fry the shrimp balls in the hot oil until golden brown, approximately 3 minutes. Drain and serve with chili paste.

Plum sauce or Chinese mustard are also good with the shrimp balls.

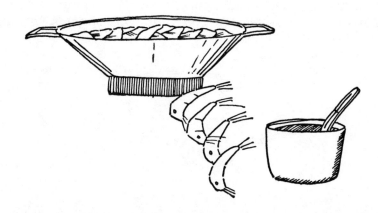

HOT AND PUNGENT SOUP

Oil for deep-frying
¼ cup raw pork, shredded (about 2" long)
2 tablespoons plus 1 teaspoon cornstarch
1 tablespoon white wine vinegar, or to taste
1½ tablespoons sugar, or to taste
½ teaspoon MSG
½ teaspoon salt
½ teaspoon white wine

½ teaspoon black pepper
¼ cup shredded bamboo shoots
¼ cup shredded wood ears, soaked according to package directions
¼ cup sliced fresh mushrooms
¾ cup shredded tofu (bean cake)
1 egg, lightly beaten
1½ teaspoons sesame oil

1. Heat the oil until almost smoking in a wok or skillet. Toss the shredded pork with 1 teaspoon cornstarch and deep-fry for 10 seconds. Remove from the oil and drain on paper towels.
2. Heat 3 cups water to boiling in a medium saucepan. Dissolve the remaining 2 tablespoons cornstarch in a small amount of water; keep at hand. Add the vinegar, sugar, MSG, salt, white wine, black pepper, bamboo shoots, wood ears, mushrooms, and tofu to the boiling water. As soon as the mixture returns to a boil, remove from heat and add the cornstarch mixture.
3. While stirring, pour in the beaten egg and sesame oil; the egg will break into shreds. Add the pork. Taste for seasoning. If you wish the soup to taste more sweet or sour, add more sugar or vinegar to taste.

THE WOK

MOO SHU PORK

Oil for deep-frying
¾ pound raw pork, shredded
1 tablespoon cornstarch
1 egg, lightly beaten
4 cups shredded cabbage
¼ cup shredded bamboo
   shoots
¼ cup sliced mushrooms

1 teaspoon sugar
½ teaspoon MSG
2 tablespoons soy sauce
1 teaspoon sesame oil
   Moo shu pancakes
   Hoisin sauce

1. Heat the oil almost to smoking in a wok or heavy-bottomed skillet. Toss the shredded pork with the cornstarch and fry for 10 to 15 seconds, or until just cooked through. Remove from the wok and drain on paper towels.
2. Remove all but 2 to 3 tablespoons of the oil in the wok. Still over high heat, add the beaten egg and stir quickly and constantly. When partially cooked but still soft, add the vegetables. Continue to stir-fry until the vegetables are crisp-tender.
3. Add the sugar, MSG, and soy sauce and stir well. Add the pork and sesame oil and toss lightly. Cover.
4. Steam the pancakes in a bamboo or metal steamer until hot and soft. Spread with hoisin sauce to taste, place a dab of the cooked pork mixture in the center, and roll up. Serve with extra hoisin sauce on the side.

Moo shu pancakes may be purchased at Chinese groceries.

HUNAN BEEF

1 *tablespoon plus 1½ teaspoons cornstarch*
1 *egg, beaten*
6 *ounces flank steak, thinly sliced*
1 *cup vegetable oil*
½ *pound broccoli*
2 *green onions, chopped*
2 *tablespoons sugar*

2 *tablespoons white wine*
3 *tablespoons Chicken Stock (see index)*
½ *cup soy sauce*
1 *tablespoon sesame oil*
1 *teaspoon MSG*
1 *teaspoon ground black pepper*

1. Dissolve 1 tablespoon cornstarch in 3 tablespoons cold water. Combine with the egg in a medium bowl; add the sliced flank steak and marinate in the refrigerator for several hours or overnight.
2. Heat the oil in a wok or heavy-bottomed skillet over high heat. Remove the beef from the egg mixture with a slotted spoon; add to the wok and stir-fry until light brown.
3. Add the broccoli and stir-fry until bright green. Remove the broccoli and beef; drain.
4. Remove all but 2 tablespoons of the oil from the wok. Add the green onions and stir-fry 1 minute.
5. Whisk together the sugar, wine, remaining 1½ teaspoons cornstarch, chicken stock, soy sauce, sesame oil, MSG, and pepper. Add the mixture to the green onions and stir briskly.
6. Return the beef and broccoli to the wok. Toss lightly to coat with the sauce and turn out onto a heated platter or bowl. Serve immediately.

Marinating the beef in the egg mixture serves to tenderize it as well as enhance its flavor.

HOT AND SPICY SHRIMP

½ pound prawns (25 to 30
   count per pound)
2 tablespoons cornstarch
1 egg white
½ cup vegetable oil
½ cup diced white onion
¼ cup sliced water chestnuts
½ teaspoon salt

½ teaspoon MSG
1½ tablespoons sugar
2 tablespoons white wine
1 teaspoon white wine
   vinegar
1 tablespoon tomato ketchup
¼ to 1 teaspoon crushed
   red pepper

1. Shell, devein, and rinse the prawns. Dry on paper towels. Mix 1 table-spoon cornstarch and the egg white together. Put the prawns in a medium bowl and pour the cornstarch/egg white mixture over them. Toss thoroughly. Marinate overnight or for several hours.
2. When ready to serve, heat the oil in a wok or heavy-bottomed skillet until very hot. Add the prawns and stir-fry, tossing constantly, until the shrimp just begin to turn pink.
3. Add the onion and water chestnuts and continue to stir-fry. Continue cooking only until the onion is soft and shrimp are bright pink. Remove all from the wok with a slotted spoon or wok spoon and drain on paper towels.
4. Mix together in a small bowl the salt, MSG, sugar, white wine, vinegar, ketchup, and crushed red pepper to taste. Pour into the hot wok and bring to a boil.
5. Dissolve the remaining cornstarch in 2 tablespoons water. Add to the sauce and mix well. Return the shrimp to the wok, toss thoroughly to coat with the mixture, and serve immediately on a heated serving platter.

THE WOK

SHI HU DUCK

⅔ cup soy sauce
1 duck, rinsed and dried
7 cups vegetable oil
3 green onions, chopped
4 thinly sliced rounds of
   fresh ginger
3 tablespoons hoisin sauce
6 pieces star anise
½ teaspoon salt

½ teaspoon MSG
1½ teaspoons sugar
1½ teaspoons cornstarch
1 teaspoon sesame oil
½ cup broccoli florets
½ cup snow peas
½ cup sliced bamboo shoots
½ cup sliced carrot

1. Spread ⅓ cup soy sauce on the duck. Heat 6 cups oil in a wok or heavy-bottomed dutch oven and deep-fry the duck over high heat, turning occasionally to allow equal browning all around. When the duck is golden brown all around, remove from the oil and drain. Strain and reserve oil for future use.

2. Mix together the chopped green onions, sliced ginger, remaining soy sauce, hoisin sauce, and anise. Spread this all over the inside and outside of the duck. Steam the duck for 1½ hours. Remove the duck from the steamer and set it aside on a plate, covered with foil to keep it warm. Reserve the steaming liquid.

4. In a medium bowl, mix together the salt, MSG, sugar, cornstarch, and sesame oil.

5. Toss the broccoli, snow peas, bamboo shoots, and carrot in the cornstarch mixture.

6. Heat the remaining 1 cup vegetable oil in the wok. Quickly stir-fry the coated vegetables in the oil over high heat until the broccoli turns bright green. Remove from the oil, drain briefly, and pour over the duck.

7. Serve immediately, carving the duck at the table and being sure to give each person a portion of vegetables.

FRIED ROSE BANANA

1 egg
2 tablespoons flour
2 tablespoons cornstarch
2 ripe, firm bananas, each
   cut into 6 pieces

1½ cups plus 1 tablespoon
   vegetable oil
1 cup sugar
1 tablespoon sesame seeds

1. In a small bowl, mix the egg, flour, cornstarch, and 1 tablespoon water until a smooth paste is formed. Thoroughly coat each banana piece with the paste.
2. Heat 1½ cups oil in a wok or heavy-bottomed pan and deep-fry the coated banana pieces until golden brown. Remove and drain.
3. In a separate saucepan, heat the remaining 1 tablespoon oil. Add the sugar and stir over moderately high heat until the sugar melts and becomes golden in color.
5. Add the deep-fried banana pieces and toss lightly. Sprinkle the sesame seeds over all.
6. Before serving, briefly dip the hot banana pieces, coated with the syrup, into ice water. The water will harden the sugar and make it crisp. Serve immediately.

The crunchy, sesame-coated exterior makes a delightful contrast to the soft, warm bananas inside.

RECIPE INDEX

Entrées

Salads and Salad Dressings

NOTES

DINING IN-THE GREAT CITIES

A Collection of Gourmet Recipes from the Finest Chefs in the Country

Each book contains gourmet recipes for complete meals from the chefs of 21 great restaurants.

___ *Dining In–Baltimore*	*$7.95*	___ *Dining In–Monterey Peninsula*	*$7.95*
___ *Dining In–Boston*	*8.95*	___ *Dining In–Philadelphia*	*8.95*
___ *Dining In–Chicago, Vol. II*	*8.95*	___ *Dining In–Phoenix*	*8.95*
___ *Dining In–Cleveland*	*8.95*	___ *Dining In–Pittsburgh, Revised*	*7.95*
___ *Dining In–Dallas, Revised*	*8.95*	___ *Dining In–Portland*	*7.95*
___ *Dining In–Denver*	*7.95*	___ *Dining In–St. Louis*	*7.95*
___ *Dining In–Hawaii*	*7.95*	___ *Dining In–San Francisco*	*7.95*
___ *Dining In–Houston, Vol. I*	*7.95*	___ *Dining In–Seattle, Vol. III*	*8.95*
___ *Dining In–Houston, Vol. II*	*7.95*	___ *Dining In–Sun Valley*	*7.95*
___ *Dining In–Kansas City*	*7.95*	___ *Dining In–Toronto*	*7.95*
___ *Dining In–Los Angeles, Revised*	*8.95*	___ *Dining In–Vancouver, B.C.*	*8.95*
___ *Dining In–Manhattan*	*8.95*	___ *Dining In–Washington, D.C.*	*8.95*
___ *Dining In–Milwaukee*	*7.95*	___ *Feasting In Atlanta*	*7.95*
___ *Dining In–Minneapolis/St. Paul, Vol. II*	*8.95*	___ *Feasting In New Orleans*	*7.95*

☐ CHECK HERE IF YOU WOULD LIKE TO HAVE A
DIFFERENT DINING IN–COOK BOOK SENT TO YOU
ONCE A MONTH
Payable by MasterCard or Visa. Returnable if not satisfied.

Please include $1.00 postage and handling for each book.

☐ Payment enclosed $_____ (total amount)

☐ Charge to:

Visa # _____ Exp. Date _____

MasterCard # _____ Exp. Date _____

Signature _____

Name _____

Address _____

City _____ State ____ Zip _____

SHIP TO (if other than name and address above):

Name _____

Address _____

City _____ State ____ Zip _____

PEANUT BUTTER PUBLISHING
2445 76th Avenue S.E. • Mercer Island, WA 98040
(206) 236-1982